▶ **Administrating Victimization**

DOI: 10.1057/9781137409270.0001

Other Palgrave Pivot titles

Pamela J. Stewart and Andrew J. Strathern: **Working in the Field: Anthropological Experiences across the World**

Audrey Foster Gwendolyn: **Hoarders, Doomsday Preppers, and the Culture of Apocalypse**

Sue Ellen Henry: **Children's Bodies in Schools: Corporeal Performances of Social Class**

Max J. Skidmore: **Maligned Presidents: The "Gilded Age"**

Lynée Lewis Gaillet and Letizia Guglielmo: **Scholarly Publication in a Changing Academic Landscape**

Owen Anderson: **Reason and Faith in Early Princeton: Piety and the Knowledge of God**

Mark L. Robinson: **Marketing Big Oil: Brand Lessons from the World's Largest Companies**

Nicholas Robinette: **Realism, Form and the Postcolonial Novel**

Andreosso-O'Callaghan, Bernadette, Jacques Jaussaud, and Maria Bruna Zolin (editors): **Economic Integration in Asia: Towards the Delineation of a Sustainable Path**

Umut Özkırımlı: **The Making of a Protest Movement in Turkey: #occupygezi**

Ilan Bijaoui: **The Economic Reconciliation Process: Middle Eastern Populations in Conflict**

Leandro Rodriguez Medina: **The Circulation of European Knowledge: Niklas Luhmann in the Hispanic Americas**

Terje Rasmussen: **Personal Media and Everyday Life: A Networked Lifeworld**

Nikolay Anguelov: **Policy and Political Theory in Trade Practices: Multinational Corporations and Global Governments**

Sirpa Salenius: **Rose Elizabeth Cleveland: First Lady and Literary Scholar**

StenVikner and Eva Engels: **Scandinavian Object Shift and Optimality Theory**

Chris Rumford: **Cosmopolitan Borders**

Majid Yar: **The Cultural Imaginary of the Internet: Virtual Utopias and Dystopias**

Vanita Sundaram: **Preventing Youth Violence: Rethinking the Role of Gender and Schools**

Giampaolo Viglia: **Pricing, Online Marketing Behavior, and Analytics**

Nicos Christodoulakis: **Germany's War Debt to Greece: A Burden Unsettled**

Volker H. Schmidt: **Global Modernity. A Conceptual Sketch**

Mayesha Alam: **Women and Transitional Justice: Progress and Persistent Challenges in Retributive and Restorative Processes**

Rosemary Gaby: **Open-Air Shakespeare: Under Australian Skies**

Todd J. Coulter: **Transcultural Aesthetics in the Plays of Gao Xingjian**

Joanne Garde-Hansen and Hannah Grist: **Remembering Dennis Potter through Fans, Extras and Archives**

Ellis Cashmore and Jamie Cleland: **Football's Dark Side: Corruption, Homophobia, Violence and Racism in the Beautiful Game**

Ornette D. Clennon: **Alternative Education and Community Engagement: Making Education a Priority**

Scott L. Crabill and Dan Butin (editors): **Community Engagement 2.0? Dialogues on the Future of the Civic in the Disrupted University**

Martin Tunley: **Mandating the Measurement of Fraud: Legislating against Loss**

DOI: 10.1057/9781137409270.0001

palgrave▸pivot

Administrating Victimization: The Politics of Anti-Social Behaviour and Hate Crime Policy

Marian Duggan

Senior Lecturer in Criminology, Sheffield Hallam University, UK

and

Vicky Heap

Lecturer in Criminology, Sheffield Hallam University, UK

palgrave
macmillan

DOI: 10.1057/9781137409270.0001

First published 2014 by
PALGRAVE MACMILLAN

Palgrave Macmillan in the UK is an imprint of Macmillan Publishers Limited, registered in England, company number 785998, of Houndmills, Basingstoke, Hampshire RG21 6XS.

Palgrave Macmillan in the US is a division of St Martin's Press LLC, 175 Fifth Avenue, New York, NY 10010.

Palgrave Macmillan is the global academic imprint of the above companies and has companies and representatives throughout the world.

Palgrave® and Macmillan® are registered trademarks in the United States, the United Kingdom, Europe and other countries.

ISBN: 978–1–137–40928–7 EPUB
ISBN: 978–1–137–40927–0 PDF
ISBN: 978–1–137–40926–3 Hardback

A catalogue record for this book is available from the British Library.

A catalog record for this book is available from the Library of Congress.

www.palgrave.com/pivot

DOI: 10.1057/9781137409270

Contents

DOI: 10.1057/9781137409270.0001

Foreword

In 1988 Maguire and Pointing (1988: 1) wrote:

> Fifteen years ago, it would have been difficult to find any-one in Britain working in either criminological research or in any agency connected with criminal justice, who gave the problems of crime victims more than a passing thought. The primary interest then was in the motivation of the offender. The victim was simply a source of information about the offending behaviour, or a witness when the case was heard in court. Yet today there is a fast growing research literature on the needs and rights of victims.

▶ Since the early 1970s, a period editors Maguire and Pointing were reflecting on, 'victims of crime' research and literature have proliferated and the victim is no longer the forgotten player in the criminal justice system (CJS). The year 2014 is a highly apposite time to write a commentary on victim policy in the UK. With the recent exposure of child sexual exploitation by predatory individuals and organized groups, high-profile cases of sexual abuse and discoveries of historical abuse, the rights, needs and welfare of victims are rarely far from the media spotlight. None of these necessarily suggests the victim of crime has regained centre stage. My task here is to introduce you to, and contextualize, the main points of *Administrating Victimization: The Politics of Anti-Social Behaviour and Hate Crime Policy.*

The focal point for this book is ostensibly 2010, and the formation of the current Coalition government by David Cameron (Conservative Prime Minister) with Nick Clegg (Liberal Democrat Deputy Prime Minister) who jointly

DOI: 10.1057/9781137409270.0002

set out the Coalition's programme of policies over the next five years (Cabinet Office, 2010). Apart from a fleeting reference to a 'Victims' Surcharge' there is no specific mention of victim policy in any section of this document including the programme for 'Justice', 'Crime and Policing' and 'Social Action'. Nevertheless, Duggan and Heap contend that the Coalition has co-opted victims and victimization, emulating a tactic employed under New Labour which they suggest was advantageous for vote-winning purposes. They argue that the Coalition's redefining and hierarchization of victimization has led to enhanced levels of individual, community and organizational responsibilization, in line with broader neoliberal ideologies.

Victims of crime have a rapidly changing role in the CJS in England and Wales and, at the time of writing, rarely a week goes by without reference in the media to changes in victim policy whether this be measures to protect witnesses in court or vulnerable victims, rights to review decisions by the Crown Prosecution Service (CPS), new guidelines for prosecutors of cases of child sexual abuse and exploitation or the appointment of new public figureheads such as the Victims' Champion, Commissioner and Minister or the publication of a New Victims' Code (2013). From a position some forty years ago when victims were acknowledged to be the forgotten people, largely overlooked in the CJS, it is now commonly accepted that victims and victim policies have moved, if not to centre-stage, at least onto the main agenda of criminal justice policy. Several changes to the UK CJS have led to an increasing visibility and engagement with victims after decades of concentrating mainly on offenders. Many changes have been introduced, particularly since 1990, aimed at (perhaps a rather over simplistic) re-balancing of the system in favour of victims (and, by implication, at the expense of offenders). Victims have been increasingly afforded greater visibility and participation in crime prevention, prosecution and punishment.

This burgeoning of theorizing, research, policy and practice related activities has enhanced the resources available to scholars, researchers, policy makers and practitioners interested in knowing about and understanding the causes of criminal victimization, its nature and extent and the policy context and practice in relation to working with victims of crime. For me, as a criminologist with an interest in a gender sensitive victimization agenda, an inter-disciplinary victimology offers some brain teasing conundrums about the gendered nature of crime and victimization and has allowed my colleagues and I to explore some very

DOI: 10.1057/9781137409270.0002

vexing and challenging social justice questions about official landscapes of victimization, hidden and dismissed experiences of victimization and the impact of victimization upon social divisions in society. What constitutes victimization and definitions of victimhood are highly contested and should always, in my opinion, be problematized.

Influences, besides the edited volume referred to above, that shaped my own appreciation and understanding of who victims are and which victims are visible in criminal justice arenas include the seminal work of Nils Christie. His oft-cited article 'The Ideal Victim' (1986) remains ever useful in understanding present common sense and popular conceptualizations of victim–offender relations. Alongside Smart's (1977) exposure of assumptions in mainstream criminology resulting in particular understandings and images of the female offender and the female victim of crime, these influences are amongst those that shaped my own growing interest in gender, crime and victimization. However, at the same time that Smart published 'Women, Crime and Criminology', Christie had 'Conflicts as Property' published in the *British Journal of Criminology*. In this article he suggested that the state has 'stolen' the crime – crime representing a conflict between offender and victim – by taking over the functions of prosecution and sentencing and excluding the victim from the process. The abstract of this article is reproduced below in full with the aim of kindling reader's interest in critically examining forty years of victim-oriented policy change.

> Conflicts are seen as important elements in society. Highly industrialised societies do not have too much internal conflict, they have too little. We have to organise social systems so that conflicts are both nurtured and made visible and also see to it that professionals do not monopolise the handling of them. Victims of crime have in particular lost their rights to participate. A court procedure that restores the participants' rights to their own conflicts is outlined. (Christie, 1977: 1)

The idea that formal criminal justice represents the theft of conflicts, removing responsibility for resolving conflict from the parties involved, connects with a critical perspective of 'the powerful'. Juxtaposing these ideas has inspired my current research inquiries into the needs of, and support for, families of child sexual abuse and doing justice for vulnerable victims. In this research hierarchies of victimization are illustrated and shown to play out in terms of victims who are, and others who are not, supported via official policy and practice developments. It also illustrates

DOI: 10.1057/9781137409270.0002

how vulnerability is a poorly understood and interpreted concept in the context of the CJS. Children and young people who have experienced sexual violence, exploitation and/or physical abuse, have mental health problems or learning difficulties (often as a result of institutionalization) comprise a large vulnerable victim group who are denied access to the CJS or fail to progress through it without being re-victimized. Although the police have increasingly adopted a victim-focused approach and the CPS now claim they adopt a merits-based approach, focusing on the overall case, ignoring myths and stereotypes rather than dwelling exclusively on the credibility of the victim, there is little evidence of vulnerable victims successfully accessing or proceeding confidently and with satisfactory outcomes, through the CJS.

Though there is little academic research on the 'justice gap' for vulnerable victims there is some evidence in connection with the approaches taken by police and prosecutors, that many complaints of victimization from those deemed vulnerable are no-crimed, dismissed or sifted out, or, 'alleged victims' are put on trial as non-credible victim-witnesses. Prosecutorial approaches currently allow for the dismissal of accounts from vulnerable victim-witnesses. Keir Starmer QC, Director of Public Prosecutions before he stepped down in October 2013, has suggested there is a category of vulnerable victims left unprotected by the law ...' (Starmer, 2013: 2) and suggests a legislated and mandatory approach is warranted to achieve a collective national consensus and cultural shift in the way the CJS treats victims of crime.

What follows in this book is a critique of institutional developments concerning victims and the provision of victim-related activities in the UK, specifically, the role of the government in setting up or coordinating victim-related activities. A distinction can be made between three potential stages of victims' experiences. Stage 1 covers from the time the offence occurs to the time the case is closed or a suspect charged. Here the primary responsibility for victim-related activities lies with the Home Office, police and non-governmental organizations providing victim support. Two government initiatives in 2012 significantly impact upon the role of the police. First, the Police Reform and Social Responsibility Act 2011 which lead to the election of Police and Crime Commissioners (PCCs) who were tasked with a responsibility for public funding of victim services and assessing police response to victims; second, Consultation Paper CP3/2012 and the reformulation of the Victim Charter. Stage 2 is the period up to, and including, trial. Here

DOI: 10.1057/9781137409270.0002

the primary responsibility for victim-related activities lies with the Ministry of Justice and Home Office, with the Witness Service provided by Victim Support. A second example of the way in which government agencies have primary responsibility for victim support during the court stage concerns Victim Personal Statements (VPSs). A third example of government involvement is through the provision of victim compensation. Stage 3 is the post-trial period which saw a statutory victim contact scheme introduced in 2004 for victims of offenders convicted of certain sexual and violent offences and sentenced to imprisonment for twelve months or more.

These three stages of a victim's experience, despite significant yet often piecemeal changes to victim policy, remain useful when considering both the reconceptualization of the victim of crime generally and when exploring the politicization of victimization and the politicizing of victims in the Coalition years. Victims, in this view, have become an important currency for political parties seeking to appear in control of crime and justice. Between them Duggan and Heap persuasively argue that some of the changes made to the criminal justice process in recent years have been cosmetic, and are the result of politicians' attempts to remain favourable by pleasing the voting public rather than to make real improvements to the treatment of victims. The remainder of this book addresses these stages of politicization through meta level themes in relation to victims, responsibilization, local-level policy developments over the past decade aimed to empower victims and communities, critiques of action and contradictions and displaced governance within the context of a wider neoliberal responsibilization policy agenda.

For me, being especially interested in the ways in which hierarchies of victimization and victimhood are constructed alongside conceptualizations of vulnerability, this book shows how such hierarchies of victimizations are used as a politicized policy package. Furthermore, the nature of relationships between victims and offenders, conceptualizations of vulnerability and the good victim, I suggest, are key features of a failure to do justice for vulnerable victims and help explain the problem of attrition. These views also connect with the responsibilization agenda for public services and welfare reforms. What follows is a bold and timely assessment of the victim as politicized and of the politicization of victimization more generally. The authors' allegations in this respect are borne out of careful unpicking of the 1990s' policy developments under New Labour and the subsequent Coalition government. They have selected a starting

DOI: 10.1057/9781137409270.0002

point which is politically pertinent and contemporarily relevant. They focus on the here and now but look backwards to understand the legitimization of non-victim focused policy developments. In this respect this book gets to the heart of a much needed debate about victim policy in the twenty-first century and reminds us of a number of already existing, but still unresolved, questions about the nature of victim policy changes. Are changes based upon a misunderstanding of the nature of victimization and victim offender relations? Are changes cosmetic gimmicks which can result in victims of crime being re-victimized, and the result of politicians' attempts to please the voting public rather than to make real improvements to the treatment of victims? This book is a statement about the implementation of victim policy, about the appropriateness of response and effective resources allocation. The provocative title of this book opens up debates that ought to be of interest to a wide-ranging demographic. It begs a recurring question: Is the victim of crime, as in the early 1970s, simply a source of information about the motivation of the offender, or a witness when the case is heard in court? Ultimately this book is a statement about the political vulnerability of crime victims. In this sense, this volume is unique.

Pamela Davies

DOI: 10.1057/9781137409270.0002

Preface

It's fair to say that this book emerged as a result of a series of coincidences. When Vicky joined Sheffield Hallam University in 2012, Marian was designated as her 'buddy' to help settle into the Department. We had been independently working on papers related to victim policy in our own research areas before realizing that there was an element of crossover between Vicky's work on anti-social behaviour (ASB) and Marian's on hate crime and domestic violence. Our theorizing and critical assessment of victim policy under the Coalition is also informed by the various interactions we have each had with victims, their representatives and the organizations which provide assistance and information. By independently engaging in 'grass-roots' work within the victims' arena, we have been witness to the ways in which policy decisions work on the ground and the potential problems seemingly 'victim-focused' directives can have on those they are designed to assist.

Upon recognizing the similarities in our work, we decided to explore the links between policies a little further, which led us to submit a panel of papers to the British Society of Criminology Conference in Wolverhampton (2013). The reception our presentations received from the audience was very positive. Whilst at the conference we both met independently with Palgrave Macmillan to discuss different potential projects and it wasn't until a few weeks after the conference that it dawned on us that a Palgrave Pivot book would be the way forward as we wanted to capture the immediacy of some of the issues

DOI: 10.1057/9781137409270.0003

victims are currently facing. We were delighted that Dr Pamela Davies, who had attended and joined in the discussions at the panel, kindly accepted our invitation to write the Foreword to this book. Her input during the process has been invaluable in honing our critique regarding contemporary incarnations of victim policy.

DOI: 10.1057/9781137409270.0003

Acknowledgements

Marian and Vicky would like to extend a special thank you to several people who assisted at various junctures with the production of this text: Dr Pamela Davies, who offered invaluable support, guidance and suggestions during the planning stages; Dr Dave Moxon and Dr Hayden Bird, who provided informative comments on drafts as the book progressed; Professor Majid Yar, who very kindly provided positive feedback in his review of our submission; Harriet Barker from Palgrave Macmillan, who guided us smoothly through the publication process; and Sumiyya Shafiq, for chairing our British Society of Criminology conference panel where the idea for this book first emerged.

Marian thanks her mum Mary and brother Del and all her mates, north and south, for their continued support and regular, much-needed, pub-based distractions from the laptop.

Vicky thanks her Mum and Dad for their unrelenting encouragement ("onwards and upwards, Victoria"), and Sam for generally being brilliant.

DOI: 10.1057/9781137409270.0004

About the Authors

Marian Duggan is Senior Lecturer in Criminology at Sheffield Hallam University, UK. Her research focuses on gender, sexuality, hate crime and targeted victimization. Marian has published widely in these areas and is the author of *Queering Conflict: Examining Lesbians' and Gay Men's Experiences of Homophobia in Northern Ireland* (2012) and co-editor of *Values in Criminology and Community Justice* (with M. Cowburn, A. Robinson and P. Senior, 2013).

Vicky Heap joined Sheffield Hallam University in 2012, having completed her ESRC CASE funded PhD investigating public perceptions of anti-social behaviour. Vicky's most recent work on ASB has focused on the 2011 English Riots, and the ASB/Hate Crime Nexus.

List of Acronyms

ACPO	Association of Chief Police Officers
ASB	anti-social behaviour
ASBI	anti-social behaviour injunction
ASBO	anti-social behaviour order
BCS	British Crime Survey
CSEW	Crime Survey of England and Wales
CJS	criminal justice system
CPS	Crown Prosecution Service
CrASBO	Criminal (or post-conviction) Anti-Social Behaviour Order
CrimBOs	Criminal Behaviour Orders
IPASB	Injunctions to Prevention Anti-Social Behaviour
IPNA	Injunctions to Prevent Nuisance and Annoyance
PCC	Police and Crime Commissioner
UKIP	United Kingdom Independence Party

DOI: 10.1057/9781137409270.0006

Introduction

Abstract: *The Introduction outlines the current socio-political context which underpins the modern perspective on victim policy developed throughout the book. An initial discussion of the political climate explores the Coalition government, their neoliberal agenda and some of the unprecedented changes being made to the criminal justice system. This context provides the foundation for discussing the aims of the book, which focus on the key question of:* How has a politicization of victimization impacted on recent victim-focused legislative and policy developments? *An overview of the politicization of victimization is then explored to consider the political imperatives of pursuing a victim-focused agenda, before the central policy domains of anti-social behaviour and hate crime are introduced.*

Duggan, Marian and Vicky Heap. *Administrating Victimization: The Politics of Anti-Social Behaviour and Hate Crime Policy*. Basingstoke: Palgrave Macmillan, 2014. DOI: 10.1057/9781137409270.0007.

This book analyses the socio-political context in which particular groups of victims have been prioritized by UK policy makers as requiring enhanced or targeted services in the past two decades. It seeks to assess the extent to which certain forms of victimization, or demarcated groups of victims, have been used by governments to further punitive political agendas under the guise of being 'victim-focused' or 'victim-led'. In doing so, the book explores the changing role and status of the victim in contemporary criminal justice discourses, as well as the increased processes of managerialism evident in facilitating victims' engagement in the broader criminal justice system (CJS).

In this Introduction, we outline the aims, context, rationale and focus of the book. Although historical context is given where necessary, the focus of the book is to develop a perspective on modern victim policy. We have adopted this approach for two central and related reasons. First, the current Coalition government exists as a political necessity yet comprises of two ideologically different parties, neither of whom have historically focused on 'victims' as a specific target group. Second, with the forthcoming 2015 general election, the dominant party of the Coalition, the Conservatives, may be shifting their focus towards 'the victim' in order to win over the electorate as part of their objective to assume total power through a majority vote.

Our critique is rendered timely when one considers the neoliberal informed socio-political and socio-economic changes evident in the UK, specifically within the domain of criminal justice. The UK criminal justice system is currently undergoing an unprecedented change; the ever-expanding privatization agenda which began with policing and prisons has rolled out to encompass offender management and victims' services. Many areas of criminal justice are being put out to tender or rewarded through a 'payment by results' system (Senior, 2013). The incorporation of victims' services within this shift indicates a reconceptualization of victims as *consumers* as opposed to service users. If this is the case then it is possible that enhanced political considerations of victims and victimization are fuelled more by economic imperatives than empathy.

Other aspects of the neoliberal agenda concern the impact of social changes on the way in which individuals are increasingly required to manage their own lives (individualization) in a context of increasingly devolved responsibility from the state to public and private agents (responsibilization), particularly within a law and order context

DOI: 10.1057/9781137409270.0007

(Garland, 2001). Much of the scholarly focus on the impact of neoliberalism has concentrated on the crime control and community safety; analysing it from a *victim* perspective illustrates shifts in the victim's role and status which affects their engagement with the criminal justice process. Drawing on Garland's (2001) depiction of the punitive turn evident in Western states during the latter decades of the twentieth century, the analysis of victim policy presented in this book explores in more depth the degree to which measures lauded as 'victim-focused' are populist, punitive and politicized. Furthermore, keeping this 'victim-focused' trajectory in mind, we address this salient point made by Garland (2001: 143) that when victims are 'given a voice', 'the voice they are given is not necessarily theirs, having been carefully stage-managed to ensure that it fits the political message of which it now forms a part.'

There has been a strong political rhetoric concerning victims, vulnerability and available means of redress evident in popular discourse recently and this is likely to continue in the lead up to the 2015 general election. This book explores political developments in victims' policy, in particular differing criminal justice approaches to seemingly similar forms of victimization. In doing so, it demonstrates how processes of individualization and responsibilization are evident in responding to victims based on demarcated *categories* as opposed to *experience*. Taking the legislative and policy domains of anti-social behaviour (ASB) and hate crime – newly categorized forms of existing types of victimization based on socio-cultural changes within the past two decades – the analysis explores the degree to which *these* victims in particular have been co-opted to further punitive political agendas. One example can be found in the Government's 'victim-focused' proposal towards enhanced criminalization and punishment for repeat or targeted victimization; common characteristics in cases of ASB and hate crime. A focus on victims is to be welcomed when the aim is to address their needs and wants, but caution is needed when these objectives are situated in a punitive paradigm.

This book emerges at a time characterized by several important factors: the 'age of austerity', cuts to the public sector, extended periods of recession, the tendering out of public services to private companies, the rise in market-based approaches (for example, to education and healthcare) and political uncertainty in the wake of a general election. The current Conservative–Liberal Democrat Coalition government is one of necessity; the Conservatives will be looking to win back voters, not least those

DOI: 10.1057/9781137409270.0007

who appear to have defected to the UK Independence Party (UKIP) since 2010. In light of these factors, this book also explores the contemporary convenience in deflecting attention away from less favourable socio-political and socio-economic issues and instead towards victims and victim policy.

Aims of the book

Several core themes inform the critique outlined in this book, all of which arose from our consideration of the following question: *How has a politicization of victimization impacted on recent victim-focused legislative and policy developments?* In exploring the answer to this question, and what impact such politicization might have had on the changing role and status of the victim in society and the CJS, our investigation can be broken down into these four key aims:

1   To explore how neoliberalism has impacted on the individualization and responsibilization of victims and their advocates in the criminal justice system;
2   To examine the nature, impact and efficacy of current socio-political approaches to addressing victims' needs and wants;
3   To evaluate whether the prioritization of repeat and targeted victimization is a conduit to advance punitive, as opposed to preventative, anti-social behaviour and hate crime policies; and
4   To assess whether the Coalition's 'divide and conquer' approach to victimization has reconceptualized victims along hierarchical lines and widened the gap between rhetoric and reality when it comes to 'putting victims first'.

The remainder of this Introduction provides an outline of how 'politicizing victimization' has been conceptualized in scholarly domains and the framework of analysis it offers to those seeking to critically examine political developments in victim policy. Following this, an assessment of anti-social behaviour and hate crime victimization provides an indication of why an enhanced policy focus on these particular domains may prove politically salient. Finally, the section concludes with a detailed chapter overview which provides an outline of the remainder of the book.

DOI: 10.1057/9781137409270.0007

Politicizing victimization

An overview of the origins and developments of victimology is outlined in Chapter 1, but for the purposes of the Introduction, a summary of the political imperatives of being victim oriented is briefly addressed. Claims that victimization, particularly criminal victimization, could be *politicized* first arose with Miers (1978) who illustrated the emergence of this process during the 1960s – a time of the civil rights movement, increasing consumerism and a growth in victim-oriented services. These services were often directed towards groups of victims, groups whose safety and security political leaders enthusiastically supported (particularly during election time) as a tactic to win popular favour in both the United States (Elias, 1990, 1993) and the United Kingdom (Williams, 1999). Therefore, the growing politicization of victimization during the twentieth century was fuelled by both grass-roots and governmental perspectives.

Elias' work has been particularly notable in analysing how official crime policy shifted focus from offenders to victims during the Reagan and Bush administrations – a period which was heavily informed by right-realist notions of crime control resulting in extensive new legislation being enacted on the premise of addressing victims' needs, rights and services (Elias, 1993). Where possible, specific groups of victims were concentrated upon in political and media discourses; when no discernable groups were available for co-opting, then a generic focus on victimization would suffice, particularly during periods characterized as economically tenuous (Mawby and Walklate, 1994). Two decades on, little appears to have changed. Statistically it is young, economically disadvantaged *men* who are more likely to be the victims (as well as perpetrators) of crime (Home Office, 2013), yet rarely are these men featured in popular discourse as 'victims', of crime. If anything, theirs is the go-to image of the perpetrator of crime and deviance. Those with the greatest fear of crime and victimization remain women, the elderly and children; thus the symbolism of these identities as constituting legitimate 'crime victims' continues to be employed in popular discourses (Davies, 2007).

A growing political concern with – and for – particular victims of crime as being *symbolic* in socio-political contexts has become more evident in law and order policies (Garland and Sparks, 2000). Claims that 'victimization and vulnerability have been socially constructed to serve

DOI: 10.1057/9781137409270.0007

political and economic interests' (Green, 2007: 91) have been supported
by suggestions that victims' policies in UK have 'sometimes seemed to
have little to do with the expressed needs of victims themselves and
more to do with other politics' (Rock, 1990: 34). Policies pertaining to
women, children and the elderly represent this populist type of focus.
On the other hand, similar approaches have been adopted by victims'
groups, where single or special interest cohorts have succeeded in securing special considerations or selective policy responses (Harding, 1994).
In such cases, politicizing victimization may be equally as strategic but
for alternative purposes. Special considerations on the basis of gender
(for example, targeted funding for women's refuges) may be indicative of
tailoring resources and responses to need, which happens to be greater
for one gender than another. However, whilst early or grass-roots victims' advocates may have been initially fuelled by good intentions (such
as feminists seeking to put hidden forms of women's victimization on
the socio-political map), separating out victims may lead to divisions in
policy responses which then would impact on the unequal distribution
of resources according to which group is best represented (or visible) in
a socio-political context.

Therefore, the contemporary co-opting of particular groups of victims
by ministers seeking to further enhance punitive crime policies requires
further exploration, as 'the symbolic figure of the victim has taken
on a life of its own, and plays a key role in political debate and policy
argument' (Garland, 2001: 144). Resurrecting Howard Becker's (1967)
question of whose side victimologists (or indeed, anyone with victims'
interests in mind) should be on, Elias (1994: 14) suggests that:

> Victimologists typically take the victim's side yet often countenance poli-
> cies in the name of victims that actually contradict victim interests. This is
> because we typically take the victim's side against the offender when instead
> we should be taking the victim's side against a much more serious barrier
> to the victim's well-being: officials and the state. This does not mean we are
> faced with some sort of intentional, state conspiracy against victims; rather
> it only suggests that official priorities necessarily lie elsewhere, buried
> under the rhetoric.

Whilst we agree that advocating a victim-focused perspective is sometimes necessary, we are also mindful that this may be used to further
right-wing or right-realist criminalization policies that are not supported by victims or their advocates, or which may have various negative
impacts on victims. Moreover, the implementation of such policies may

DOI: 10.1057/9781137409270.0007

necessitate a victim first being created in the first place, greatly contradicting the preventative element which ought to be underpinning such objectives. Evidence that this may be occurring forms part of our critical appraisal regarding if, and how, the management of victims and victimization forms part of broader electoral strategies to capitalize on the fear of crime from a different angle.

Our analysis of the above political manoeuvres is concentrated on two specific areas of policy: ASB and hate crime. Although victim identities have shifted considerably over the past two decades to the point where 'a wider array' of victims is more evident (Hall, 2010: 59), specific ASB and hate crime victim identities have been constructed and are now recognizable in both policy and popular (media) discourse. Certainly, both domains have generated a fair share of media coverage as being symbolic of the need to address victimizing behaviours which can cause repeat distress for those subjected to them. In the case of hate crime, an enhanced media focus on particularly serious, fatal cases (or their subsequent investigation, trial and outcome) have led to recognizable names indicating the potential danger of hate motivated victimization. The murders of Stephen Lawrence, Jody Dubrowski, Ian Baynham, Anthony Walker, Brent Martin and Fiona Pilkington are some of the more notable victims variously affiliated to hate crime and ASB behaviours.

The development of nuanced language, ideologies and guidelines concerning engagement with ASB or hate crime victims means they may be dealt with differently in respect of their experience or identity. Policy responses exist to address these forms of victimization accordingly, but may result in a potential hierarchizing *among* and *between* these two cohorts as a result of various additional factors. The following section provides a brief rationale for focusing the analysis of enhancements in the politicization of victimization on ASB and hate crime specifically.

An overview of ASB and hate crime

Contemporary understandings of victimization have not emerged in a vacuum, nor have they remained static over time. The study of victims, their identities and experiences have been subject to scrutiny from a variety of perspectives and produced a number of different ideologies, typologies and responses. However, Kearon and Godfrey (2007) note

DOI: 10.1057/9781137409270.0007

that it was in the last quarter of the twentieth century when 'the victim' began to be mobilized in a range of diverse and often contradictory or mutually exclusive narratives, public debates and policy initiatives. Various Victims' Codes of Practice addressed the treatment of victims in the CJS as a homogenized group, juxtaposed against 'the offender'. Soon, however, identity constructions around the 'victim of crime' became increasingly fragmented. Reconstructions of 'the victim' have been evident along increasingly complex lines of (among other things) identity, experience, harm incurred and impact (Mawby and Walklate, 1994). Whilst problematic in some respects, the categorizing of victims according to experiences or encounters allows for the targeting of resources, policies and interventions to the needs and wants of that particular group.

Our analysis of victim policy in this book concentrates on two such categories: ASB and hate crime, which also comprise of comparatively recent areas of critical scholarly analysis. The explosion of an ASB discourse in the late-1990s not only blurred the boundaries between civil and criminal conduct but also led to an increased 'net-widening' and 'mesh-thinning' of criminal justice (Cohen, 1979). Much of the academic scholarship which ensued addressed the criminalization of young people, or those on the peripheries of the criminal justice system at risk of being drawn further in through a political redefining of criminal perimeters. Victim status has evolved in this area, closely mirroring developments in ASB policy itself. Originally enacted to provide respite for victims suffering noisy or nuisance neighbours, ASB has transformed into an area which currently focuses on protecting vulnerable and/or repeat victims from a wide range of ASB types, and which – interestingly – from 2014 has included hate crime for the first time.

Hate crimes refer to offences based on the perpetrator's prejudice towards the victim's actual or perceived identity category. The legislative and policy approach adopted by New Labour to tackle specific forms of targeted victimization initially covered race, religion, sexual orientation and disability (gender identity was later added by the Coalition government in 2013). Importantly, the nature of the incident dictated how it was responded to, and all of this was dictated by the identity of the victim(s). Ironically, the identity characteristics now used to demarcate and protect vulnerable victims are the very same factors once used to persecute such minorities (for example, through slavery laws and segregation, or the criminalization of homosexuality and mental illness). On the whole,

DOI: 10.1057/9781137409270.0007

however, hate crime policies indicate that there are discernable victims who may be targeted on the basis of their actual or perceived identity; that these victims are blameless with regards to their victimization; that they and their experiences can – and should – be recorded and responded to differently from other forms of crime; and that the responsive (as opposed to preventative) legislation and policy should focus on the individual offender and act as opposed to the wider structural factors and environment in which the hate crime occurs. In essence, the current responsive criminal justice system seeks to increase hate crime reporting rates in order to prosecute more offenders, rather than address the causal factors informing hate crime to prevent it occurring in the first place.

These areas of ASB and hate crime victimization are linked in several ways: they may be experienced by a victim more than once, thus may produce 'repeat victims' or instances of 'repeat victimization' by virtue of the types of incidents experienced or individuals targeted. They each encompass types and levels of victimization which can be viewed as existing on a 'continuum' (Kelly, 1988; Stanko, 1990). This can vary from verbal abuse, intimidation, minor assault or criminal damage through to acts which result in serious violence or death. Often, early intervention at the 'lower' end of the scale can prevent the victimization increasing in severity, but may require some level of criminal justice input. Incidents at the lower end of the continuum may not be recognized or reported for similar reasons: perhaps it is the first occurrence; perhaps the victim has minimized the harm or damage done, or explained it away with reference to perceived situational or causal factors; or perhaps such incidents have become part of the tapestry of their everyday interactions, thus raising the benchmark for what is deemed to be noteworthy victimization.

However, these two forms of victimization are considered separately in political policy – police recorded data and victimization surveys. Such specificity may be commendable on some levels, allowing for greater involvement and engagement with otherwise marginalized or 'hard to reach' communities or victims who are reluctant to come forward to report their experiences. If an incident or crime fails to show up in police or victimization statistics, it may not be deemed an area of social concern, thus result in little political impetus to address the issue. However, being subject to separate policy guidelines means focusing on the identification of, engagement with and desired outcomes for victims *according to these crime types*. In other words, being identified as a victim of either ASB or hate crime will affect how the CJS responds (in terms

DOI: 10.1057/9781137409270.0007

of investigation, charge, sentence, victim support or services). This may occur in two very different ways even though the type of victimization experienced is likely to be very similar. As we have argued elsewhere (Duggan and Heap, 2013) and will expand upon further in this book, a separatist approach may prove *politically* advantageous (being seen to as doing more for different groups of victims), yet without careful consideration, inconsistencies and errors may abound which could ultimately prove detrimental for the most vulnerable in society. Further pitfalls include the breeding of discontent among those who perceive victim 'hierarchies' to exist, or see some groups in society as receiving 'special treatment' from criminal justice agencies.

Chapter outline

This final section provides an overview of the aims and objectives informing each chapter. Chapter 1 provides a framework for conceptualizing victims. The aim of the chapter is to present an overview of the changing role and status of the victim in research and theory, with some reference made here to policy and practice. The discussion begins by charting how victims came to prominence in both scholarly and political domains, analysing the origins of, and developments in, victimology (the study of victim and victimization). This then informs the evaluation of how such scholarship influenced the construction of victim categories or identities, attributable to victim types. Processes of governance and their impact on victims and their advocates are analysed next, using Foucault's concept of governmentality as a theoretical framework within which to address the relationship between the victim and the state. This theoretical perspective is then applied to the final section of the chapter, a closer look at how processes of individualization and responsibilization have shaped contemporary notions of victimization and, in turn, the development of policies related to the process of managing the victim experience.

Chapter 2 explores the notion of victims as vote winners. The aim of this chapter is to present the recent socio-political context in which policies and practices concerning victims have emerged. Beginning with an overview of the origins and nature of the present Coalition government, a focus on the neoliberal agenda and its impact on victims' services in the UK provides a basis from which to address the enhanced politicization of victimization. In adopting a critical approach to examining the

DOI: 10.1057/9781137409270.0007

political rhetoric concerning victims, the analysis turns to the establishment of victims' 'figureheads'. The earlier themes of governance and responsibility are invoked to assess the impact of these figureheads on victims' role and status in the CJS from a positive (enhancing victim visibility) and negative (enhancing victim bureaucratization) perspective. This 'politicization' critique informs the final section which suggests that a strategic co-opting of victims' issues may be warranted in light of a need to deflect public attention away from a growing media interest in 'political deviance'. The final section discusses deviancy and social change addressing this from a political (government ministers' engagement in fraudulently claiming expenses) and social (online harassment and bullying) perspective.

Chapter 3 adopts a prioritized focus on ASB and hate crime policy. The aim of this chapter is to investigate *contemporary* policy developments in these two areas in light of the 'victim-focused' rhetoric espoused by the Coalition government. Taking each area separately, the origins and developments of ASB and hate crime precede a critical overview of how political interventions within these forms of victimization illustrate elements of right-realist ideology in the form of enhanced criminalization or control. With regards to ASB, the near-farcical fluctuation in political responses to non-criminal forms of deviancy has been echoed by the conveyer-belt approach to defining acronyms designed to be synonymous with this particular Coalition government. Turning to hate crime, recent proposals to enhance and extend existing criminal sanctions indicate that politically convenient policy approaches to targeted victimization remain responsive, as opposed to preventative. While the symbolism underpinning such decisions may be espoused as 'victim-focused' (enhancing punishments to recognize the severity of targeting *particular* victims) the fact remains that in order for this 'symbolic gesture' to be availed of, a victim needs to be created in the first place.

Chapter 4 concludes the book by suggesting that a reconceptualization of victims and victimization has emerged during the past two decades. Drawing on the evidence presented, the chapter indicates that processes of politicization in contemporary victim policy have constructed new hierarchies of victimization. These hierarchies indicate how certain groups of victims and victimization have been subject to enhanced levels of bureaucratization within the criminal justice system, whilst others have been overlooked entirely. The chapter demonstrates that victim hierarchies have been reconstructed along three lines: *demarcation*

DOI: 10.1057/9781137409270.0007

(categorizing the victim or victimization type), *prioritization* (capital-izing on the victim or victimization experienced in a populist punitive manner) and *responsibilization* (compelling the victim to understand and navigate the CJS, or tasking victim advocates with this). This move towards processing victims and victimization in the CJS may be extolled in political rhetoric as part of a wider 'victim-focused' agenda, but is exposed in this chapter as evidence of a move towards *administrating* victimization. Rather than reduce or eliminate forms of victimization, current victim policy seeks to manage the victim experience in the CJS in line with the dominant political ideology underpinning current devel-opments in criminal justice. With that in mind, the chapter concludes by considering how victims may feature in the 2015 general election and calls for a renewed victimological focus on the impact of political proc-esses on administrating victimization.

DOI: 10.1057/9781137409270.0007

1
Conceptualizing Victims

Abstract: *Chapter 1 provides a framework for conceptualizing victims in light of victims' changing role and status in research, theory, policy and practice. The discussion begins with the origins and developments in victimology which informs the evaluation of how such scholarship influenced the construction of victim categories or identities, attributable to victim types. Foucault's concept of governmentality is then adopted as a theoretical framework within which to address the relationship between the victim and the state to address how processes of individualization and responsibilization have shaped contemporary notions of victimization and, in turn, the development of policies related to the process of managing the victim experience.*

Keywords: Foucault; governance and governmentality; ideal victim; state legitimacy; victimology; victim typologies

Duggan, Marian and Vicky Heap. *Administrating Victimization: The Politics of Anti-Social Behaviour and Hate Crime Policy.* Basingstoke: Palgrave Macmillan, 2014. DOI: 10.1057/9781137409270.0008.

Evolutions in the study of victims and victimization have produced a wealth of information about the direct and indirect effects and impacts of crime, as well as victims' and witnesses experiences of engagement with the criminal justice system (CJS). With the majority of criminal acts producing at least one discernable victim, this is a cohort which governments overlook at their peril. However, as it is clear that governments cannot guarantee the prevention of crime – and, consequently, victimization – it stands to reason that they might instead seek to address (or deflect some of the responsibility for) existing victims' expectations, experiences and needs. Some victims prove easier to manage in these respects than others, thus the separating out of people according to victimization type allows for a targeted approach to interacting with certain groups, possibly to the detriment of others.

This chapter begins the book's analysis of victim policy by focusing on two key areas. First, an overview of victimology demonstrates the evolution of victim considerations in scholarly and theoretical domains. Of particular note here is the emergence of victim typologies, which have become increasingly attached to idealized notions of 'deservedness'. The concept of deservedness divides victims along good and bad lines, with some being seen as more worthy of an enhanced criminal justice focus than others. Nonetheless, the sheer number of victims created through crime remains a pressing burden on criminal justice resources. Therefore, deflecting some of the responsibility for crime prevention onto the public not only frees up state resources, but also diverts the focus away from its failure to protect citizens in the ways in which the state is expected to. The discussion around theorizing governance and governmentality contained in the latter half of the chapter explores how victims have increasingly been constructed as stakeholders by the government. The nature and impact of this elevated status outlined here informs various aspects of analysis throughout the remainder of the book.

The evolution of victimology

This section charts the socio-political development of the victim identity, providing a historical context to the origins and development of victimology in the UK by assessing the impact of positivistic, critical and radical approaches to victims. The brief introduction to victimology illustrates the emergence of victim typologies, or categorizations. These

DOI: 10.1057/9781137409270.0008

were founded on personal characteristics or perceptions of culpability, deservedness or legitimacy depending on the types of actions or behaviours displayed. The qualities attributed to different groups of victims according to their identities, experiences or actions and behaviours give an early indication as to why some groups of victims may be prioritized by policy makers. The more blameless a victim can appear to be the easier it is to promote punitive law and order policies related to the offender. However, as will be demonstrated later, enhanced criminalization is not necessarily in the best interests of the victim.

Conceptualizing the crime victim

Unlike perpetrators of crime, or indeed the criminal justice system itself, victims of crime have not traditionally commanded much scholarly focus, attention or investigation. This may in part be due to the state acting on behalf of the victim when pursuing justice through a criminal trial. In 1976, Nils Christie delivered a speech on 'Conflicts as Property' at the University of Sheffield which was later published in the *British Journal of Criminology* (Christie, 1977). In what has become a seminal piece of writing, he argued that highly industrialized societies have formalized and mechanized conflicts to assert a guise of power and control but, whilst doing so, have 'stolen' these from the victim and their community. His paper illustrated how changes have occurred which result in the two key parties to the conflict (ordinarily the victim and offender) being represented by the state but to differing degrees, so much so that the victim is 'pushed completely out of the arena, reduced to the trigger-off of the whole thing' (1977: 3). Thus, victims may be strategically removed and reintroduced at various junctures during the criminal justice process in a manner which illustrates their malleability, usefulness and relative powerlessness. Contrastingly, by involving itself in conflicts, the state legitimizes its existence and decisions in relation to victims and offenders. In liberal democracies, it can claim to be doing this in a representative capacity, given that it has been democratically elected by the voting public.

Although a focus on victims has been historically less evident in comparison to offenders, they have not been overlooked entirely. Kearon and Godfrey (2007) provide a comprehensive backdrop against which to assess what they deem to be the 're-emergence' of the victim in academic and political debates during the mid-twentieth century. They

DOI: 10.1057/9781137409270.0008

conclude that, historically, three distinct periods characterize victims' involvement – and visibility – in criminal justice processes: their role as an 'essential actor' pre-nineteenth century, a 'symbolic actor' from the mid-nineteenth to late twentieth centuries, and as a 'fragmented actor' from the late twentieth century onwards (2007: 30–31). It was during this middle, 'symbolic' period that scholarly focus on the victim and their experience developed. However, prior analyses on offenders and offending had a strong impact on the origins and development of theorizing victims and victimization.

Ideas about crime, criminality and control rapidly developed following the Enlightenment period. Key thinkers such as Cesare Beccaria, the 'father of criminology', considered the relationship dynamics between the offender, victim, state and society when crimes occurred. In what has become known as the 'Classical' theory of crime, Beccaria noted how shifts had occurred from the Middle Ages, when the victim was central to the pursuit of justice in identifying the transgression and seeking retribution from the perpetrator *without* recourse to the state, through to a system whereby the state punished offenders without much consideration of the victim. The impact of criminological theory on a codified system of criminal justice during the onset of the Industrial Revolution indicated changes in the regulatory dynamics of society through enhanced state control and surveillance underpinned by the desire for greater discipline and power (see Foucault, 1975). The criminal justice system as it is conventionally understood (with the establishment of the police, prison and probation services in the nineteenth century) is approximately two centuries old. The foundations of this CJS were aided by developments in theories of crime which correlated with social control during a period of extensive social change characterized by advances in transportation, industrialization and urbanization. The focus on punishing offenders and preventing offences, coupled with the financial benefits that state-controlled punishment brought through fines, meant that the visibility afforded to crime victims was slowly eroded from the increasingly formalized system of justice.

Classical criminological theorizing began from the premise that the offender must be engaged in some form of rational decision making and that they were aware of what they were doing (Beccaria, 1767/1963; Bentham, 1798/1996). These ideas developed as part of the broader Enlightenment period where grand enquiries into the nature of man emerged from philosophical perspectives. This was later refuted by

DOI: 10.1057/9781137409270.0008

Darwin-inspired biological and psychological positivistic notions which addressed internal and external factors which may determine the freedom of choice regarding engagement in criminal activity (Lombroso, 1876/2006). These varied approaches inferred that crime was something that could be rationalized, measured, understood and clearly identified. With this in mind, when the focus turned to researching *victims* of crime in the mid-twentieth century, positivistic-informed theories, research and frameworks of analysis were strongly evident in the emerging victimological arena.

Five key theorists are credited with producing the sub-discipline of victimology: Benjamin Mendelsohn (1947), a Romanian lawyer working in the US; Hans von Hentig (1948), a Hungarian criminologist working in the US; Marvin Wolfgang (1957), an American sociologist and criminologist; Stephen Schafer (1968), a German-American psychiatrist; and Menachem Amir (1971), a student of Marvin Wolfang. These early victimologists sought to investigate the nature of the criminal or victimizing act, the relationship between the criminal and victim, the actions of either or both preceding the act, and the actions – if any – taken by the victim to deflect or deter victimization from occurring. This resulted in the production of victim typologies (based on the victim's identity characteristics) and classifications of victim responsibility (based on the victim's actions or behaviours) which were used to determine the level of culpability attributable to a victim of crime. An overview of these early theorists' work now follows, providing a foundation from which to analyse an apparent return to these core themes of responsibility, culpability and accounting for the victim–offender relationship.

Categorizing victims: typologies, culpability and deservedness

Benjamin Mendelsohn is credited with first coining the term 'victimology' in the 1940s to describe the growing body of scholarly work which sought to account for victimization. He, like his contemporaries, sought to attribute some level of blame or responsibility to the crime victim as well as the offender. The specific focus of this work was not to identify the needs, wants or experiences of victims, but instead to seek to identify causal factors which would both hold them to account for the crimes or harms they had incurred, and aid the development of crime prevention. The core themes of precipitation, facilitation and

DOI: 10.1057/9781137409270.0008

provocation fuelled victimological enquiry in a manner which was largely aimed at expanding knowledge about how to reduce criminal offending, rather than addressing experiences of victimization. A key factor of note is the impact of chosen research methodologies and frameworks of analysis on the social construction of victim blaming. Von Hentig, Mendelsohn and Schafer looked at a wide variety of cases to determine the nature and impact of, amongst other things, inter-personal relationships within a criminal incident as well as any relevant factors prior to, during and after it had occurred. As a result, their findings indicated that clear distinctions were drawn between *identity* factors (such as being very young or old, being female or being mentally impaired) and *situational* factors (such as being engaged in criminal conduct or the commission of a crime at the time, or provoking a criminal response from an aggressor) which went towards determining the level of culpability or blame to be bestowed upon that particular victim.

Following the production of these typologies, it was only a matter of time before specific crime types would be subjected to a closer inspection within these theoretical frameworks to learn more about criminal victimization and its possible prevention. Wolfgang's research into homicides in America was the first such study to address victim precipitation within a singular crime type. He demonstrated that over a quarter (26%) of the 558 homicides he examined in Philadelphia involved one or more of the following factors: male offenders and victims, histories of violent offending, alcohol consumption, weapon possession, and the initiation of physical violence (Wolfgang, 1957). Many of the cases began as minor altercations which escalated to homicides due to the presence of one or more of these contributing factors. This proved useful to indicate the steps which could be taken in similar situations to potentially prevent an argument resulting in a homicide. However, this study influenced one of Wolfgang's students to produce research which not only sparked controversy through the highly publicized, critical feminist backlash to the findings, but would mark the beginning of the modern victims' movement.

In 1971, Menachem Amir studied a sample of forcible rape incidents obtained from police reports in Philadelphia, USA. Using only the data obtained from the reports (and not any interaction with the victims or perpetrators themselves), he concluded that a fifth of the rapes in his sample could be described as victim-precipitated. However, unlike the

DOI: 10.1057/9781137409270.0008

homicide victims in Wolfgang's study who had been engaged in some form of criminal or semi-criminal behaviour (carrying weapons, engaging in drunken conduct, instigating physical violence), the culpable characteristics or attributes Amir outlined among the forcible rape victims in his study included: being intoxicated (with the level of voluntariness ignored); acting seductively; wearing seductive clothing; having a dubious reputation; or being seen as sexually 'available' (Amir, 1971). Crucially, however, it was Amir's assertion that such factors were determined by the (male) perpetrator, not the (female) victim, which indicated a deeply gendered power imbalance and suggested that women, not men, were responsible for policing male sexuality and sexual victimization. Unlike other forms of criminal victimization, rape and sexual violence remains one of the few crimes where the victim's reliability, credibility and potential culpability are scrutinized as closely, if not more so, as that of the alleged perpetrator.

Perhaps unsurprisingly, Amir's assertions prompted a backlash from women, many of whom were scholars and activists in the emerging second-wave feminist movement, who saw 'victim-culpability' as akin to 'victim-blaming'. Taking hold in the late 1960s, second-wave feminism focused on the needs, wants and experiences of the (female) victim, seeking to address these with the establishment of support services for women, many of whom had been physically or sexually abused by men (Cook and Jones, 2007; Hoyle, 2007). As well as shifting the focus from culpability to need, feminists challenged the propensity to measure how 'deserving' a person was of embodying a victim status. In doing so, they indicated that this particular identity – 'the victim' – had become saturated with cultural meaning which could work in a person's favour or against them. As Miers (1990: 227) outlines:

> victims of crime occupy a social role ... where they are seen not to conform to the expectations associated with it, they diminish their chances of being sympathetically treated, and may even forfeit their occupancy of the role.

Miers (1978) also criticized the ideology behind the term 'victim' as encompassing passivity and suffering. Victimology has since been critiqued for doing little to address or challenge the ideology of passivity and vulnerability afforded to victims of crime (Newburn and Stanko, 1994; Godfrey et al., 2007). This has been similarly challenged by feminists who adopted the term 'survivor' instead (Kelly, 1988; Rock, 2007).

DOI: 10.1057/9781137409270.0008

'Survivor' is predominantly used to refer to women and children who have survived abuse, most usually from men, as a way of counteracting the disempowering passivity (and elements of culpability) which had come to be associated with the 'victim' label. Survival is fluid, whereby victimhood appears static. Surviving abusive experiences also involves a greater degree of personal investment and struggle to 'come out the other side'; something not captured in the 'victim' ideology. As Spalek (2006: 26) indicates: 'Underpinning the "victim as survivor" identity is the theme of individual victim as agent who has resisted their abuse to become emotionally and psychologically stronger.'

The acknowledgement of how victimization can be assessed in terms of the 'deservedness' of the individual or their identity in addition to their experience of harm or crime is crucial in understanding perceptions of, and responses to, victims. Deservedness also forms the root of Nils Christie's (1986) 'ideal victim' thesis, which remains popular in social and political discourses around victims and victimization. Christie noted the popular conceptualization of 'ideal victims' in society, invoking particular characteristics against which deservedness of legitimate victim status was measured. Deserving victims were characterized as weak in relation to the offender (ideally female, sick, very old or very young); virtuous, or engaged in legitimate, everyday activity; blameless for what has happened to them; unrelated to the offender (this 'stranger' element also implies that it is a person, not an organization, who has committed the offence and that it is likely to be a single incident); opposite to the offender (who is 'big and bad'); and eliciting unqualified sympathy through their attained victim status. The weak, vulnerable, disempowered victim is contrasted to the strange, scary and motivated perpetrator in a way which provides clear divisions and may be used to validate increased criminal justice responses. This may prove *politically* expedient, but the degree to which these are in the *victim's* best interests is often questionable.

The concepts of typologies, culpability and deservedness have remained important areas of consideration within the victimological arena throughout the latter half of the twentieth century. Perceptions of victim culpability may enhance or reduce the 'legitimate' status afforded to a victim, potentially impacting on the services available to a person on this basis. If victims are situated on a binary against offenders *or* against one another, then problematic hierarchies may begin to emerge. Traditional notions of victim hierarchies based on the 'ideal

DOI: 10.1057/9781137409270.0008

victim' were constructed on the basis of victims' innate (and sometimes immutable) identity characteristics such as gender and age (although age changes with the individual, the concept referred to youth or old age). Contemporary incarnations of victim hierarchies may instead draw on acquired characteristics or identities. Carrabine et al. (2009: 161) suggest that those occupying the bottom end of such hierarchies are those 'whom the dominant majority in society see as troublesome or distasteful' – for example, the homeless, sex workers and those with drug or alcohol dependencies. In contrast, new formations of those occupying the top reflect the characteristics proposed by Christie (1986) above – for example, elderly victims, young children and hardworking citizens.

It is clear that in its short existence, victimology has evolved rapidly to produce a greater knowledge and understanding about the victim experience. Considerations of victims and their experiences have evolved from typologies determining their culpability to addressing levels of deservedness and vulnerability. Such processes of separation indicate how people have been 'siloed' along demarcated lines. While this may prove advantageous in some respects, such as the provision of specialist services, potential disadvantages are evident. This 'siloing' of victims according to demarcated factors may construct hierarchies based on identity or experience which is used to *infer* need, rather than being based on need itself. Ironically, those in most need may be unable to avail themselves of assistance due to not being perceived as vulnerable or eligible within this identity framework. Being at the bottom of such a hierarchy may be undesirable; being omitted altogether (for example, alcoholics, drug abusers, street sex works, vagrants) is far worse.

Focusing on those at the top of traditional hierarchies may prove politically advantageous for governments either seeking to retain, reaffirm or regain legitimacy and public favour, or to push law and order agendas in alternative, 'victim-focused' manners. An assessment of the governance of victimization now follows which indicates the ways in which power, legitimacy and autonomy function in society. These issues are then explored within the victimological domain to demonstrate their capacity to broaden out the perimeters of government into the everyday lives of citizens and the impact this has on diffusing state responsibility and accountability for addressing and responding to victimization.

DOI: 10.1057/9781137409270.0008

Processes of change in governing victimization

The observations and critique presented in this book's analysis of Coalition victim policy draw heavily on notions of power and control outlined by French philosopher Michel Foucault. In this section, Foucault's ideas are discussed before being applied to the ways in which a management of victimization has become evident. The discussion examines how fluctuations in state legitimacy can inform a move towards a greater individualization of risk and responsibility. This theme is returned to in the final chapter when the analysis questions whether such diffusions of responsibility are indicative of a trend towards lessening the state's accountability to prevent victimization, or for harms incurred as a result of victimization. The discussion contained within this section demonstrates the theoretically informed perspective from which we evaluate policy developments and directives, including the imposition of victims' figureheads (Chapter 2), the enhancement of criminalized and punitive responses to victimization (Chapter 3) and the increased responsibilities imposed upon victims and their advocates (Chapter 4).

Governmentality and social control

Foucault's analyses of power, control and discipline produced theories which addressed the relationship between forms of power and the production of knowledge, and in turn between the state and the citizen. His questioning of social control through the imposition of, and regulation through, social institutions provided a platform to deconstruct, or question, how power functions to appear natural, restrict freedoms and govern entire groups of people in discriminatory ways (see Foucault, 1975, 1979). One of the ways in which Foucault conducted this exploratory, deconstructing process was to provide a geneaological examination of the relevant factors in a given situation; to trace its origins and developments. As part of this critical method of investigation, Foucault suggests an analysis of how technologies of power function on macro (for example, the sovereign state) and micro (for example, in the home) levels to regulate or govern people either physically or psychologically. This 'technologies of power' analysis forms part of his conceptualization of 'governmentality', which he identifies as being:

> at once internal and external to the state, since it is the tactics of government which make possible the continual definition and redefinition of what

DOI: 10.1057/9781137409270.0008

is within the competence of the state and what is not, the public versus the private, and so on; thus the state can only be understood in its survival and its limits on the basis of the general tactics of governmentality. (Foucault, 1991: 103)

In other words, understanding the ways in which technologies of power may function to shape people's mentalities (for example, towards adopting a particular stance or position on a given issue) requires an analysis of the rationales fuelling this process, where the power is seen to lie, how it functions, who is affected by it, what outcomes may be produced and what alternatives might exist.

Analyses of governmentality are not limited to the sovereign, or ruling, power (most usually the government or state). However, employing a governmentality focus illustrates how the government rules through deploying its power from both a recognized hierarchical, 'top-down' structure and a less-recognized 'bottom-up' means through institutions (such as the school, factory, hospital or workplace). Individuals who are tasked with representing the ruling power, usually through the implementation of its policies, therefore become part of this wider remit of state control. As this trickles down in society, individuals at the very bottom of the chain are also affected by these dominant ideologies or policies. For some, regulation is guaranteed through self-policing (or self-regulation) or policing one another (peer-to-peer regulation). The occurrence of this furthers the ruling power's objectives in conscious and unconscious manners. Examples of this in the UK can be found in the historical legal and social regulation of sexual promiscuity or deviancy, and mental illness.

More contemporary forms of governmentality would be the economic and political shift from post-war Keynesian welfarism to free-market, neoliberal policies. Societies have been reconceptualized from groups with duties and obligations to enterprising and autonomous individuals with rights and needs. However, they are still perceived as needing to be subject to control (Garland, 2001). Individuals and their acts are subject to processes of governmentality in various ways. For example, punitive socio-political responses to particular, non-conforming acts or identities brand these as deviant, resulting in the potential creation of 'moral panics' (see Cohen, 1972). This in turn may function to shape society's ideas on law and order in line with the dominant political ideology if the fear of crime attributed to this person or act were enhanced as a result of the moral panic around them or it.

DOI: 10.1057/9781137409270.0008

The more aware people become of potential dangers around them, the more likely they are to take measures to protect themselves, or give up some of their autonomy to be protected by the state. This may be rendered more feasible if such dangers were socially constructed through discursive means thus rendered more identifiable. Anti-social behaviour and hate crime, the two areas of victim policy focused upon in this book, are examples of these 'discursively constructed' dangers. Despite not being 'new' or vastly different in terms of the nature of victimization experienced, both have been subjected to heightened and distinct levels of social and political focus. Upon achieving greater individualization, the ruling power may absolve itself of some of the responsibility for *protecting* citizens, as they have been reconceptualized as more autonomous, so concerns itself with *achieving justice* on their behalf instead. This in turn allows the ruling power to enhance crime control measures which seek to respond to harms, rather than addressing social issues (such as state reductions in welfare and public services) informing the motivations or rationales for perpetrating harm in the first place.

Concepts of governmentality assist in the development of broader understandings of where power lies and how it may function, particularly to control individuals and society. The themes of discipline and knowledge are central to these understandings. When dominant modes of power are internalized, social control is achieved through individuals engaging in process of self-governance in line with the messages which they have absorbed. Describing such processes of regulatory governance as a 'governing of the self' (or self-policing), Foucault illustrates how power does not just operate within a political sphere, but rather permeates people's everyday lives. Understanding this process is vital to explore how ideas, actions, behaviours and identities are regulated on both formal in informal bases whilst demonstrating how power is rationalized by those subjected to it. Foucault calls this analysis a focus on the 'conduct of conduct': how one conducts oneself in public, the relationships one chooses to have, the image one aims to portray are all shaped by, and go on to shape, social mores and values.

Foucault's critique also evidences the broader nature of this arrangement; the conduct of the masses reflects the state's level of governance, power and legitimacy (or lack thereof). Early modern philosophers such as Hobbes, Locke and Rousseau indicated how legitimacy is a key part of the social contract for effective governance in democratic societies. In contrast to the ideal outlined by these political philosophers, namely

DOI: 10.1057/9781137409270.0008

a predetermined social contract, the current governmental situation is instead more of a post-election political *compromise* (see Chapter 2). Nonetheless, some factors remain the same; often, the more repressive a state is, the less legitimacy it is seen to embody by those subject to its power (see, for example, the Arab Spring socio-political uprisings which began in 2010). It has not gone unnoticed that law and order agendas which promote *enhanced* levels of criminalization and punitive penal policy have usually occurred during periods characterized by *low or falling* crime rates. Such observations may be widened out to encompass victimization; reductions in crime rates have not quelled the government's enhanced focus on addressing victims of crime as in need of management. However, this has been done in a capacity which focuses on victim provision, rather than victimization prevention. In effect, remaining adamant that potential victimization is as pressing an issue as ever thus allows for an alternative or less-visible expansion of punitive penal approaches which capitalize on fears of crime and victimization.

Processes of governance: victims as stakeholders

Bache (2003: 301) defines governance as 'an increasingly complex set of state-society relationships in which networks rather than hierarchies dominate policy-making'. Crawford (1997: 6) proves a more detailed definition, suggesting that governance is:

> a pattern of shifting relations which involve: the fusion of, and changing relations between, the state, the market, and civil society; a move from 'social' to 'community'; greater individual and group responsibility for the management of local risk and security; and the emergence of new forms of management of public services and structures for policy formation and implementation.

An example of 'interactive policy making' (Mayer et al. 2005) is the level to which the public are more actively involved as stakeholders at the point of a policy's design, far ahead of its delivery or implementation. This is most usually done by putting plans or initiatives out for public consultation (in addition to inviting responses from specific advocates). The fact that past, present and potential victims are becoming stakeholders in new and unprecedented ways may be part of the broader neoliberal agenda to reduce the scope of government. Alternatively, it may be a by-product of the drive towards neo-liberalism whereby less-significant functions are willingly handed over if they tie into the larger public relation aims of

DOI: 10.1057/9781137409270.0008

the government. As will be expanded on in the following chapter, this has taken the form of privatizing various aspects of the welfare state and increasing bureaucracy and managerialism within public services.

On a more individual level this involves reconceptualizing who is responsible for the management and avoidance of risk, encapsulated in the naming of laws after victims, particularly 'ideal victims', such as legislation pertaining to the disclosure of information about child sexual offenders: 'Megan's Law' after Megan Kanka in the US, and 'Sarah's Law' after Sarah Payne in the UK. Similar laws have recently been adopted around the disclosure of information pertaining to the risk of domestic violence, named 'Clare's Law' after Clare Woods, and a campaign is currently underway for an 'Eve's Law', led by domestic abuse survivor Eve Thomas, which aims to allow victims to keep their safe house addresses secret in court. Concerns have been raised about the potential for schemes which allow people to avail of information which could then put them in a position of enhanced responsibility either by avoiding risk by taking action, or assuming culpability for not acting on the knowledge obtained (Duggan, 2012).

The state still desires to wield control, but seeks to avoid being held completely responsible for individuals. Therefore, processes of 'responsibilization' begin to remerge, whereby people perceive themselves, rather than the state, as accountable for various aspects of their lives (such as their health, employment, welfare or security). This devolution of responsibility proves politically (and economically) advantageous in lessening the state's role in providing public services. In addition, the enhanced focus on the privatization of risk-management results in individuals being cast as responsible for minimizing their risk of harm by maximizing the measures they take to engage in a care of the self (Lemke, 2001). This can be seen as expanding into the victimization domain. Deans (2010: 199) notes how the 'extraordinary political reinstatement' of the victim has manifested new forms of victim empowerment though support groups, promoting their political voice or reclaiming spaces; all, he suggests, as a result of the victims' apparent failure to manage their own risks of victimization. Taking this further, within a framework of stakeholder engagement, the victim (past, present or potential) is addressed within the logic of the dominant neoliberal ideology which is ascribed to wholeheartedly by those in positions of power.

This diffusion of responsibility through enhanced stakeholder involvement may impact on victims in ways which are further debilitating,

DOI: 10.1057/9781137409270.0008

directly as a result of interacting with the CJS. The victim's involvement with the CJS is far more extended, intensive and extensive (given the various different agencies a victim will interact with as the case progresses) thus the potential for things to go wrong at one or more of the stages is a very real concern. When this happens, it is often compared to the original experience, being described as a form of 'secondary victimization', this time at the hands of the CJS. Davies (2007: 259–261) illustrates how several measures have been put in place to lessen the chances of victims feeling used by a process which may be seen by them (and others) as more 'system-oriented' than 'victim-oriented'. The aim of these initiatives has been to ensure the victim's co-operation as the case progresses through the CJS, so as *victim*-oriented as they may first appear they are ultimately *system*-oriented. This increased focus on practice and procedure led to the establishment of the first Victims' Charter in 1990 (updated in 1996 and 2002) being replaced by the Code of Practice for Victims and Witnesses (established through the Domestic Violence, Crime and Victims Act 2004). Falling short of providing victims with rights, these enforceable sets of guidelines instead sought to manage the increasingly administrative experiences victims were required to undergo to achieve 'justice'. These, and the raft of additional measures aimed at improving service provision and delivery, indicate a shift towards governing victimization from a responsive, as opposed to preventative, standpoint.

To summarize, the development of victimology as a specific area of focus has be founded on considerations of victim types, categories, identities and culpability, leading to some victims of similar crimes being addressed differently according to their characteristics. Such considerations of victims and victimization have led to the development of categorizations which may separate and 'silo' victims according to identity or experience, tailoring assistance accordingly or focusing on hierarchies of need to promote enhanced CJS responses. Governments seeking legitimacy or validity may capitalize on victims or fears of victimization in this way to assert their authority in politically turbulent times, thus regulating populations and delivering justice. Political engagement with victims has also been demonstrated as reflecting the governmentality thesis outlined by Foucault and Garland, whereby individualized citizens are reconceptualized as stakeholders in crime and punishment objectives. Continuing in this vein, the following chapter addresses the increasing tendency towards professionalizing victims' services and politicizing victims' needs, exploring how a greater investment in victims may serve

DOI: 10.1057/9781137409270.0008

to deflect attention from current socio-political troubles afflicting the Coalition government.

Summary of key points

▸ Victimology has evolved to consider victim types, categories, identities and culpability.
▸ Some victims may be considered differently according to inherent or attributed characteristics.
▸ Processes of governance have altered the ways in which victims and their experiences are interacted with throughout the criminal justice system.
▸ Governments seeking legitimacy or validity may capitalize on victims to assert their authority in regulating populations and delivering justice.

DOI: 10.1057/9781137409270.0008

2
Victims as Vote Winners

Abstract: *Chapter 2 explores the notion of victims as vote winners to evaluate the recent socio-political context in which policies and practices concerning victims have emerged. The Coalition government's neoliberal agenda is explored in relation to its impact on victims' services and the increasing politicization of victimization. The analysis of victims' 'figureheads' invokes earlier considerations of governance and responsibility to assess the impact these figureheads have on victims. This 'politicization' critique suggests that a strategic co-opting of victims' issues may be warranted in light of a need to deflect public attention away from a growing media interest in 'political deviance' illustrated through government ministers' engagement in fraudulently claiming expenses.*

Keywords: austerity; Coalition government; deviance; neoliberalism; politicized victims; victims' figureheads

Duggan, Marian and Vicky Heap. *Administrating Victimization: The Politics of Anti-Social Behaviour and Hate Crime Policy*. Basingstoke: Palgrave Macmillan, 2014. DOI: 10.1057/9781137409270.0009.

This chapter explores several core issues informing criminal justice policy generally, and victims specifically, which have become evident during the Coalition's time in power. Taking Elias' (1986: 231) claim that 'victims may function to bolster state legitimacy, to gain political mileage, and to enhance social control', the current Coalition government's commitment to addressing victimization appears to be in line with the reconstruction of victims as consumers of criminal justice services. Beginning with a short overview of how the Coalition emerged following the 2010 general election, the evaluation concentrates on the degree to which neoliberalism and law and order politics have underpinned their approach to criminal justice. A shift in the political landscape towards a neoliberal, individualistic outlook has been commonly attributed to Margaret Thatcher's time as prime minister (Cohen, 1985; Mawby and Walklate, 1994) although this has been disputed elsewhere (Farrall and Hay, 2010). Continued political investment in victims has been evident through the privatization or tendering out of public (and victim) services; political discourses and policy formulation on specific areas of victimization; and enhanced punitive approaches to the types of victimization characterized as 'more serious' as a result of incurring repeat or targeted elements (Spalek, 2006). An analysis of established 'victims figureheads' and the current socio-political and economic climate informs the chapter's assessment of whether focusing on victims of crime and providing them with enhanced levels of visibility constitutes little more than a tactical method of deflection from less-favourable political developments.

The UK Coalition government

The current Coalition government arose following the 2010 UK general election, itself a watershed moment in British politics with regards to process (the first ever televized leaders' debates) and outcome (the first peacetime coalition for more than 70 years). The 'first past the post' British electoral system requires that a political party gains a majority number of votes to assume (or retain) power. In the 2010 general election, none of the political parties managed to achieve the 326 seats required for an overall majority, leading to the second 'hung parliament' since 1974. Despite gaining the highest number of seats, the Conservative Party was still 20 short of a majority. Following Gordon Brown's resignation as the Labour Party leader, and at Her Majesty the Queen's

DOI: 10.1057/9781137409270.0009

invitation, Conservative leader David Cameron entered into talks with Liberal Democrat leader Nick Clegg to form a Coalition government. The workings of this new arrangement were codified in *The Coalition: Our Programme for Government* (HM Government, 2010), comprising elements from each party's individual manifesto: *Invitation to Join the Government of Britain: The Conservative Manifesto 2010* (Conservative Party, 2010) and *The Liberal Democrat Manifesto 2010: Change That Works for You* (Liberal Democrats, 2010).

As a result of the Coalition coming to power in this manner, their level of mandate to govern as an elected representative of the people is subject to greater scrutiny. Unlike their predecessor Labour, whose landslide victory in 1997 was seen to give them a larger, more robust mandate, the Coalition – as a governing body established *after* the election – had to introduce several policies which addressed areas where the two parties differed in opinion (such as tuition fees, privatization agendas and electoral reform) (see Quinn et al., 2011). Blondel and Cotta (1996, 2000) have illustrated that supporting parties in coalitions are less likely than the majority party ministers to initiate policy initiatives which encourage significant social change. The more dominant party is seen to have more of a mandate and, therefore, more of an institutional obligation to address socio-economic issues. In effect, the supporting party may be there to make up numbers as opposed to wielding any real power in these arenas (Blondel and Cotta, 2000). This proves important when coalitions are seeking to present united fronts in the face of adversity, or where one party is keen to align itself to particular or popular policies.

The Coalition's continual focus on austerity and the supposed need for public sector cuts have dominated its four years of government thus far. Many of the socio-economic policies have been implemented at a scale and speed that have been described as 'risky' and as putting considerable strains on the Coalition on economic, political and social levels (Taylor-Gooby, 2012: 66). The impact of these cuts on vulnerable people has been routinely highlighted by social campaigners, with many stating that changes to benefits in particular will damage living standards for some of the poorest groups, as well as increase levels of poverty and inequality (Taylor-Gooby, 2012). The Liberal Democrats have appeared largely powerless to soften the blow, seeming instead to focus on their own agenda of (failed) electoral reform.

Since 1979, the Conservative Party has been affiliated to punitive law and order policies which seek to clearly separate victims from

DOI: 10.1057/9781137409270.0009

offenders with a view to focusing on punishing rather than preventing crime. The Liberal Democrats, by comparison, have been less vocal in criminal justice matters. Although neither have focused much on victims of crime in the past, there is a *current* shift towards this cohort, whether past, present or potential victims. This harmonious focus can be seen as benefiting both parties of the Coalition. Although it is in the interests of *any* political party to be seen as being on the victim's side and promoting policies aimed at benefiting the needs and wants of victims, the policies being espoused by the Coalition appear to be illustrative of the more punitive law and order stance associated with the Conservatives. The Liberal Democrats, who would normally be reluctant to align with such traditionally right-wing ideological positions, appear more amenable when these discourses are situated within a victim-focused paradigm.

Neoliberalism and victims' services

A strong characteristic of the Coalition government has been its commitment to the ongoing neoliberal agenda. Neoliberalism can be characterized as method of political organizing which draws heavily on ideologies rooted in economic justifications. A particular emphasis is placed on the effective management of public resources within a framework of competitive markets. Linked to this is the promotion of more liberal, deregulated economic arenas coupled with an enhanced focus on privatizing publicly owned assets. With regards to modes of governance, neoliberalism espouses greater levels of individual autonomy, self-regulation and a delegation of responsibility (or 'responsibilization') that reduce the level of direct state intervention into subjects' lives. The following discussion provides an overview of how the neoliberal era has impacted on victim services in light of David Cameron's vision of a 'Big Society' and the marketization of service provision.

The impact of neoliberalism on *victims* is an area in constant development, owing to both the broad nature of services required and those provided. The trend towards co-opting victims in the market sector was first noted by Heilbroner who stated:

> Vested interests from politicians, pressure groups, charities, insurance companies, the security industry and housing developers all suggest that victims are one of the most recent groups to become subject to the logic of capitalism. (Heilbroner, 1985 cited in Green, 2007: 107)

DOI: 10.1057/9781137409270.0009

In 2013, the Ministry of Justice produced a guide for the commissioning of victims' services (Ministry of Justice, 2013). Stating that this was a 'strategic move towards more personalized services for local people' (ibid.: 5), the report outlined the devolution of most services to locally elected Police and Crime Commissioners (PCCs) whilst the Ministry of Justice would retain responsibility for specific areas including commissioning the support services for victims of domestic and sexual violence. The report also suggests there should be a targeting of services to victims who have suffered the greatest impact, chiefly victims of serious crime (including rape and sexual violence), those who are persistently targeted and those deemed to be vulnerable or intimidated – interestingly denoted as those 'likely to become victims' as opposed to already experiencing victimization (Ministry of Justice, 2013: 6). The funding available to PCCs for the commissioning of these services was outlined in section 56 of the Domestic Violence, Crime and Victims Act 2004, although additional legislation is currently being drafted by the Secretary of State to provide further clarification on PCC's powers of provision. This will include the ability to provide services for those affected by anti-social behaviour not directly caused by a criminal offence; currently, this group of victims are excluded from the funding issued under section 56 of the 2004 Act although other monies available to PCCs may be used to address such victimization (Ministry of Justice, 2013).

The Ministry of Justice report identifies eight principles of good commissioning, which include understanding user needs and seeking user feedback; active engagement with third-sector organizations to avail of their specialist knowledge; consulting local experts; being outcome-driven; striving for transparent, fair (and where possible long term) contracting processes; and, interestingly, sharing risk (Ministry of Justice, 2013: 13). Identification of local victims' needs will be the responsibility of that area's PCC, as will an assessment of existing services offered to victims to see if there is scope for a merging of service provision (ibid.: 18). Underpinning the evaluation of service provision are two core outcomes: 'helping victims first to **cope** with the impact of crime, and subsequently to **recover** from the harm they have experienced although not all victims will return entirely to the lives they had before' (ibid.: 21, original emphasis). *Outcomes* are differentiated from *outputs* in that they are perceived as being victim-focused, denoting 'changes, benefits, learning or other effects that happen as a result of services and activities provided by an organisation' (ibid.: 22). Suggestions of how to measure these outcomes

DOI: 10.1057/9781137409270.0009

include obtaining information regarding the service user's quality of life as well as feelings of safety or fear at entry and exit points. Successful commissioning, according to the report, is based upon user satisfaction and not just take-up rate, albeit an equally strong focus is placed on 'securing value for money' (ibid.: 5). The money in question is provided either through a grant or a contract, with the decision ultimately resting with the individual PCC. While recognizing the procedure of determining whether grants or contracts are to be awarded is a complicated one (subject to European Union Treaty and procurement obligations), the report merely distinguishes larger services (valued at or above £113,057) from smaller ones; no indication is given to how different organizations might be interacted with to boost their chances of bidding for grants or contracts.

Charitable and private (for-profit) victim-focused organizations share similar traits in terms of needing a secure, assured and ongoing 'clientele' base in order to legitimize their existence. Wong (2013) depicts a pertinent difference between the two, noting that the community voluntary sector is scrutinized to a lesser degree by social and political commentators as a result of being judged on their values and desire to assist those they encounter. The offset of this, however, is that this sector is less financially equipped to tender for the increasing number of public service contracts being made available by the Coalition. Just 1 per cent of the larger community voluntary sector organizations have annual incomes in excess of £5 million (which equates to two-thirds of the share of total annual income across all charities), meaning that they are currently unable to compete with the public and private sector to bid for contracts (Wong, 2013: 282). The continuation of specialist, charitable organizations being in a position to provide expert help to victims is in increasing danger as a result of economics trumping ethics under a Coalition agenda.

Albertson et al. (2013) provide an economic evaluation of the criminal justice system and in doing so highlight several important points with regards to how costing out crime and victimization impacts on political decision making. Although their analysis is focused primarily on offending, the difficulty in accurately defining the costs of victimization in the UK is further complicated through 'the impact of crime on potential victims manifesting as fear of crime' (Albertson et al., 2013: 318). Albertson et al. warn that assessments concerning the 'cost to the community' prove difficult, thus are 'effectively missing from the cost of crime estimates currently used' (ibid.: 319). Attempts by Victim Support to do exactly this reiterated these inherent difficulties. In 2000, the Home Office's inclusive estimation of the cost of *crime* to England and Wales for the preceding year stood at £60 billion with over half (£32 billion) attributable to crimes against individuals and households (excluding motoring offences) (Brand and Price, 2000). Taking Albertson et al's (2013) indication that the consequences of crime on indirect victims cannot effectively be accounted for, the complexity (not to mention potential size) of these costs becomes increasingly apparent. This in turn begins to shed light on the ever-expanding privatization agenda in an age characterized by discourses of 'austerity' and government cuts. This agenda would perhaps make more sense if the country were in the grip of spiralling crime rates; however, the opposite is in fact true. Crime has been *falling* for two decades. Various statistics, both official (when police recorded crime statistics were characterized as such) and large-scale victimization surveys have noted a gradual decrease in recorded crime since the 1990s; 58 per cent since 1995 (ONS, 2014).

The impact of criminal victimization survey findings on shaping criminal justice policy is an integral focus of analysis for many scholars, as retaining such a strong focus on CJS policy is indicative of the crisis in legitimacy outlined above. Criminal victimization surveys first emerged in the United States in 1967; the UK followed suit in 1977 with an initial survey by Sparks, Genn and Dodd which soon led to the establishment of the British Crime Survey (or BCS, now the Crime Survey for England and Wales or CSEW) (Walklate, 2007: 4). These have proven useful not only for charting trends in crime and victimization, but also for driving political agendas. Crime statistics are vulnerable to manipulation with regards to their production and findings, being amended accordingly in line with particular political aims. According to Mayhew and Hough (1988), findings from the first British Crime Survey were downplayed in light of a growing public concern around crime and the apparent inability of the government to control and reduce levels of offending. A decade later, such manipulation appeared less necessary given that police recorded crime began to fall markedly since its peak in 1992, and victimization surveys since their peak in 1995. Despite these drops, CJS crime reduction policy remained heavily focused on offence-led strategies linked to routine activity theory (Cohen and Felson, 1979); for example, the Reducing Burglary Initiative (see Hamilton-Smith, 2004). Future comparisons between police and victimization surveys may prove difficult with the recent decision by the Office for National Statistics to

DOI: 10.1057/9781137409270.0009

withdraw the police's gold-standard 'national statistics' status as a result of repeated allegations that some of the quarterly published figures were subject to 'a degree of fiddling' (Travis, 2014).

Contemporary CJS policy is being pursued under very different circumstances. By the time New Labour came into power in 1997, crime rates had been falling for two years. When the Coalition was established, crime rates had been falling for almost two decades. According to the Office for National Statistics (2013), police recorded crime has fallen by 7 per cent compared to 2011/12, reaching the lowest level since new recording measures were introduced in 2002/03. Victim based crime fell by 9 per cent to constitute a rate of 55 per 1000 population, which accounts for 83 per cent of police recorded crime. When taking specific offences into consideration, reductions were seen across all offence types apart from theft from the person (9% increase), sexual offences (1% increase, which has been attributed to the 'Jimmy Savile effect'[1] whereby victims of historic sexual abuse now disclosing their experiences), harassment (13% increase), trafficking for sexual exploitation (19% increase), soliciting for prostitution (11% increase). Related closely to harassment, 'personal' ASB, where ASB is deliberately targeted at an individual or group, represented 28 per cent of ASB incidents recorded by the police, which equates to 644,000 incidents. This is a vast number when considering a lot of ASB remains unreported (Heap, 2010). From this, alongside other well-established criticisms of police recorded crime, we can suggest there are even greater numbers of victims of ASB. Taking victimization into consideration, the 2012/13 CSEW reports a 9 per cent reduction in overall crime on the previous year, which has resulted in the lowest level since the inception of the BCS in 1981, halving the amount of crime from the 1995 peak (Office for National Statistics, 2013). This has been emulated with regards to the number of victims recorded, albeit with some caveats according to the nature of certain types of victimization. The 2011/12 survey, for example, showed there were 536,000 victims of sexual assault in the past year and 2.0 million of domestic abuse, indicating little variation in numbers over the past decade or so (ibid.).

CJS policy making in a crime-drop context is not new, as the New Labour government elected in 1997 faced a similar situation (albeit to a lesser extent in their first term in office). Mooney and Young (2006) suggest New Labour established the ASB agenda as a means of taking the initiative on law and order in light of falling crime rates towards the end of 1990s. The analysis provided above suggests that similar tactics are

DOI: 10.1057/9781137409270.0009

evident with the Coalition's current focus on victimization, again during a time of falling crime rates. Exploiting the political capital of victims by prioritizing them generally as a group (or certain victims specifically) demonstrates an ideological difference from New Labour and represents a populist policy to tempt the voting public.

Politicizing victimization

In the period leading up to the 2010 general election, David Cameron made a concerted effort to 'soften' his and his party's image in line with a more socially liberal approach, both visually (often being seen in casual wear or without a tie) and ideologically (diverting political rhetoric away from tax, immigration and the European Union) (Quinn et al., 2011). However, Cameron's attempts to come across as a 'man of the people' have been undermined by the significant number of policy U-turns in the past four years. This indicates that during the policy formation period at least politicians are out of touch with the public, often amending proposals following negative responses. Shelved plans affecting the justice sector alone have included scrapping the Youth Justice Board; granting anonymity to defendants in rape cases; limiting payments under the criminal injuries compensation scheme so that only seriously injured victims would be eligible; and attempting to scrap plans to remove violent partners from the home (reinstated after a significant backlash from women's groups) (Owen, 2013). The Coalition, in particular the Conservative Party, is losing popularity. Information from available opinion polls at the time of writing indicated that the Conservatives were consistently trailing Labour in points, whilst the Liberal Democrats were regularly being pushed to fourth place by relative newcomer, the UK Independence Party (UKIP) (BBC News, 2014).

With a 2015 general election looming, the Coalition's interest in victim policy has emerged through their political pledge to '(re)focus on the victim'. This focus falls short, however, of providing victims with rights. Instead, they have continued with the established trend of setting out guidelines (via Charters and Codes of conduct) as issued by previous governments to address the needs and wants of crime victims as identified by various victims' organizations. These guidelines have also evolved from demarcating victims as a homogenous group to specifying particular types of crime victim or victimization. The most recent incarnation along these lines was the Code of Practice for Victims of Crime,

DOI: 10.1057/9781137409270.0009

produced by the Ministry of Justice in December 2013. The Code forms part of the *Criminal Justice Strategy and Action Plan*, launched in June 2013 and promising a more transparent and preventative criminal justice system. As well as providing updated information concerning what people should expect from each stage of the criminal justice system, the Code pays particular attention to the provision of services to victims of 'the most serious crimes' which are depicted as including hate crime, domestic violence, terrorism and sexual offences, persistently targeted victims and all vulnerable and intimidated victims. Commenting on the Code, Secretary of State for Justice Chris Grayling MP stated: 'I want to create a fairer criminal justice system where victims have a louder voice and those who break the law are more likely to go to prison for longer. I also want to ask everyone working with victims to help deliver the promises in the new Code and make sure their needs are put first' (HM Government, 2013b).

Furedi (1998: 82) claimed that 'in an increasingly fragmented society, social solidarity and belonging is achieved through the shared responses to victims and victimization'. Equally of note is Currie's (2010) observation that crimes which involve tangible or visible harms may be seized upon by governments seeking to enhance popular punitive responses as part of a law and order agenda. As has been demonstrated above, victim visibility in the CJS has fluctuated according to reasons usually outside of the victims' control. Hall (2010: 3) outlines two particularly pertinent areas of enquiry for contemporary analyses of victim policy: victims' concerns as relevant to the criminal justice process and victims' interests as goals in their own right. Left-realist theoretical perspectives (Lea and Young, 1984; Lea, 2010) suggest examining the realities of 'hidden' forms of victimization and government responses to these in order to indicate the extent to which considerations of certain victims prove politically advantageous as part of wider vote-winning tactics.

Discourses pertaining to victims have traditionally conceptualized them as a *homogenous* group, sharing the experience of being affected by crime and dichotomously contrasted against being an offender. However, renewed perspectives regarding victims have begun assessing their needs or wants according to how their victimization has been demarcated. Political aspirations for enhanced criminalization and sentencing have not been based on the severity of the behaviour or act demonstrated by the offender, but instead on the victim's identity characteristics or experiences of being repeatedly targeted. These enhancements 'pathologize'

DOI: 10.1057/9781137409270.0009

individual offenders as seeking to cause more or greater harm to specific individuals, ignoring the effect or impact of wider social or political structures informing or sustaining their prejudices. However, rather than addressing issues of social or structural deprivation, racism, homophobia, vulnerability and so forth, categorizing victims and suggesting that they need special treatment serve a political purpose in deflecting attention towards what appears to be more positive efforts to address victimization.

Politicians variously invoke socio-economic factors (as well as individual fallibility) as influencing criminality, yet the policies they promote fail to focus more robustly on social interventions which may function to *prevent* more crime from happening. This is counterproductive to reducing crime and victimization but does allow for a justification of criminal justice policies. As Currie notes, societies which have 'set out to reduce inequalities of class and gender, to provide more generous social supports for vulnerable families and individuals, to counter the dominance of market relationships and imperatives generally, are less wracked by serious violence than those that haven't' (Currie, 2010: 116). DeKeserdy and Schwartz (1991: 250) note that it is not generally in governments' interests to make links or address wider social and economic policies, especially where there is a lingering pathologization of the individual which allows for those deemed criminal to be effectively demonized. The impact socio-economic factors can have on levels of street or visible crime would undermine the criminal justice imperatives being pushed by the ideological right, and the move towards law and order policies in the sector. Seeing crime as an issue located in the individual, as opposed to society, gives further credence to such stances. As will be examined in Chapter 3, rather than addressing social or cultural factors underpinning hostility which would offer greater protection from targeted or repeat victimization, the formation of responsive legislative and policy changes seek to punish offenders *more harshly* instead. This may well align with the ideological perspectives of the right, but those more likely to be affected by crime and criminal victimization may not share these sentiments.

The prioritizing of criminal justice responses to social problems (often addressed within ASB discourses) are illustrative of what Stan Cohen described as 'net widening' and 'mesh-thinning', through the device of 'pre-emptive criminalisation' of sub-criminal activities (Cohen, 1985). This is harmful to victims as it relies upon victimization to occur (in

DOI: 10.1057/9781137409270.0009

order to discern both the crime and the 'victim' from the 'offender') for the response to ensue. As many victims of 'lower level' or minor yet repeated infringements attest, the police can do little by way of an intervention until this level of victimization is deemed significant. This draws the victim into the CJS process earlier and with more interaction, therefore indicating a move towards greater levels of policing and victim agency involvement in what Lea (2010: 148) terms a process of 'authoritarian renewal':

> In the process democratic accountability is replaced by mobilization of 'respectable' elements – those with secure jobs and property who define themselves as the community and as collective potential victim while the marginalized are externalized as a risk group. In these situations the social relations of crime control are weak to the point of non-existence.

DeKeserdy and Schwartz (1991) suggest there is a culture of 'vague populism' which is concerned with crime control policies being rooted in the community. However, it may be within these very communities that racism, sexism and classism may be informed and sustained through poorly implemented community control or prevention crime strategies. Furthermore, the notion of 'community' can be a problematic one as gatekeepers may operate as additional barriers to justice for those whose voices are marginalized even further. Forms of community silencing may be more notable within some types of victimization (such as domestic violence within minority communities), so care needs to be taken to ensure that alternative routes are available to represent myriad experiences within a given community.

Victimization has also undergone processes of politicization through the auditing measures increasingly imposed which seek to address victims' levels of satisfaction with the services they receive. Research into victim satisfaction with the CJS has highlighted problems regarding mismatches between victims' expectations and the procedural nature of the system (Shapland et al., 1985; Jordan, 2001). However, although victim satisfaction rates are used as 'a proxy measure' against which to measure the success of a range of criminal justice provisions, in some cases different services may yield different responses according to the level of deservedness affiliated to the particular victim (Hall, 2010: 5). Victims with more status, or seen to be less culpable, may avail of better services than those lower down the scale or seen as somewhat complicit in their victimization. With expansion of victim 'types' or

DOI: 10.1057/9781137409270.0009

'categories' according to harm experienced, victim identity or nature of act, it would appear that a more tailored service is being offered at the entry level of the CJS, particularly in relation to reporting hate crime. Procedural differences can take the form of recording data to highlight specific elements of a case; offering specialized victim support services based on the victim's identity; enlisting restorative justice mediators to intervene; or pursuing a particular form of prosecution designed to focus on the targeted identity. These criminal justice procedures may be subject to policy interventions in order to manage victim expectations and increase overall satisfaction rates as part of the 'victim-focused' shift in political strategizing.

More difficult to ameliorate is the fear of repeat victimization. In a survey conducted by the Probation Service into what victims want from sentencing, the majority (94%) cited the non-commission of further offences as being the most important thing, with four in five (81%) victims preferring sentences to be effective in achieving this desistence rather than being focused on harsher punishments (Ministry of Justice, 2007). Between 1998/9 and 2007/8 the Labour government increased spending on law and order from £17.9 billion to £32.5 billion, a 46 per cent increase in real terms (The Centre for Social Justice, 2009). Further evidence of a punitive turn was also illustrated by the exponential rise in the prison population, doubling in number since 1992 to routinely set record highs for the number of inmates held at any one time. This had very little impact on reducing the fear of crime or victimization among the general public. Studies show that 43 per cent of the UK population consider crime and violence to be one of the most worrying issues in their lives, considerably higher to comparable areas such as Germany (21%) and America (27%) (Duffy et al. 2008). A key reason for this is the daily diet of crime stories promoted by popular media sources, where the focus on serious and violent crime vastly outweighs its actual occurrence. However, if it is this type of crime which is seen to be most feared, or most anticipated, then it stands to reason that policies relating to victims of such crimes prove attractive to politicians seeking to make their mark in an electoral race.

Political rhetoric capitalizing on populist social issues has proven to be a successful tactic for governments in fighting and winning elections. While policies relating to law and order have usually centred on targeting crime and punishing criminals, in light of the aforementioned crime drop, new forms of victimization have proliferated in political discourses,

DOI: 10.1057/9781137409270.0009

coupled with a renewed focus on tackling existing forms from fresh directions. Shifts towards a greater emphasis on addressing victimization (specific types of victimization in particular) may be illustrative of politicians devising an alternative route to uphold their 'strong on law and order' ideologies. The following section explores how successive governments have sought to operationalize victim-focused rhetoric by enlisting victims' figureheads and gradually bestowing greater visibility – but not power – to these delegated roles.

Establishing victims' figureheads

Central to Coalition victim policy is the endorsement of figureheads designed to promote 'the victim's voice' through enhanced visibility in social, political, legal and criminal justice arenas. Victims' voices, however, are increasingly being channelled through representatives whose discourses emulate the retributive political sentiments of the dominant power. As Garland (2001: 143) notes, 'the voice [victims] are given is not necessarily theirs, having been carefully stage-managed to ensure that it fits the political message of which it now forms a part.' This may be rendered less noticeable through the enlisting of real-life victims, co-opted as a result of their media celebrity or activism in the victims' movement. The following section draws on Garland's analysis to provide an overview of the changing nature of several victims' roles, exploring their affiliated status, claims to power and achievements in order to assess what it is victims are 'saying'.

The Victims' Champion

Over the past five years, victims have been variously represented by several figureheads, each with a demarcated role and purpose. This began in 2009 with the establishment of a Victims' Champion, designed by New Labour, to provide an independent voice to victims and witnesses in the criminal justice system. The Champion had the following remit: to listen to the concerns of victims and witnesses; to represent their views to government officials and in the media; to challenge criminal justice agencies further to reform practices for victims and witnesses; and to prepare foundations for the appointment of a Victims' Commissioner in 2010, a proposal which had been outlined as part of the Coroners and Justice

DOI: 10.1057/9781137409270.0009

Bill and was under review by parliament at the time the Champion's role was established (BBC News 2009).

In January 2009, Sara Payne was appointed as the first Victims' Champion. Payne had become a prominent child protection campaigner and media figure after her eight-year-old daughter Sarah Payne was murdered by paedophile Roy Whiting in 2000. Working closely with a national newspaper, Payne had previously campaigned for a scheme which allows members of the public to seek information from the police about individuals who have contact with children where the child's safety is of concern. The Sex Offender Disclosure Scheme, also known as 'Sarah's Law', was rolled out nationally in 2008 following a successful pilot period of four areas. It is based on using information on past sexual offending with a view to preventing future victimization. Guidelines instruct the police on how, and to whom, this information can be disclosed on the basis of the relationship of the enquirer to the child (Kemshall et al., 2010). The Scheme works in tandem with the Multi-Agency Public Protection Arrangements (MAPPA), which are designed to ensure public safety by managing sex offenders in the community and to provide clearer rules around what information can be shared about an individual, and to whom disclosures can be made.

During her time as Victims' Champion, Payne conducted a wide-ranging review of the criminal justice system, producing a report on this in 2009 (which no longer appears to be available online). Information about the report (a lot of which is available online) indicates that her suggestions included clearer information regarding sentencing so that victims were aware of when offenders were likely to be released. She also highlighted the lack of criminal justice support for people affected by anti-social behaviour, particularly that which was seen as criminal in nature by the victim. There was a particular focus on victims' counselling needs and dearth of available services to address these, as well as improving complaints procedures for those dissatisfied with the service. In terms of tangible outcomes, the justice secretary at the time, Jack Straw, pledged the first national Victims Service which would offer the bereaved relatives counselling and access to free legal advice. However, the current incarnation of this Victims' Service appears to comprise a single webpage on the Ministry of Justice website (last updated in March 2011) which provides a link to Victim Support (established in 1974). Although Victim Support was awarded £8 million a year to deliver the service, no information is available regarding the needs of families bereaved by homicide

DOI: 10.1057/9781137409270.0009

(Victim Support Website, 2010). When Payne's report was published, the chief executive of Victim Support at the time, Gillian Guy, was cited as calling it a 'missed opportunity' due to the fact that: 'It doesn't tackle the problem that however much we tweak the justice system to help victims and witnesses, we are trying to make it do something it was not designed to do' (Morris, 2009). Ultimately, this fundamental point still stands; the CJS is primarily concerned with processing offenders, therefore victims are in danger of being 'processed' in a similar manner if efforts are made to make them fit the system better rather than the other way around.

The recommendations outlined by Payne appear to have been addressed in a somewhat lukewarm fashion by the incoming Coalition government in comparison to her second report into rape victims' experiences in the CJS (Payne, 2009). The recommendations from this second report have informed the government's policy commitment to End Violence against Women and Girls. It is possible that the timing of Payne's earlier, wide-ranging recommendations may have been their downfall; the implementation of a national Victims' Service may have been quietly dropped as a result of being associated with the former political regime. If so, then further exploration is needed into *which* victims are prioritized according to which government produced the relevant initiative.

The Victims' Commissioner

One of the objectives of the Victims' Champion had been to pave the way for the incoming Victims' Commissioner, a post which had been created under the Domestic Violence, Crime and Victims Act 2004. Therefore, the failure to extend the Champion role past its 12-month remit, or install a new Champion, was due to the emergence of this alternative victim figurehead position. Comprising of a greater degree of power and authority, the Victims' Commissioner was tasked with a statutory duty to actively promote the interests of victims and witnesses in the CJS, encourage good practice in their treatment and regularly review the Code of Practice for Victims, which sets out the services victims can expect to receive.

In March 2010, Louise Casey was the first person appointed to this role, occupying this position until 2011. During her time in the post, Casey centred on specific areas of victimization, focusing in particular on victims' needs for counselling and emotional support and the treatment

DOI: 10.1057/9781137409270.0009

of bereaved families. She produced a report which called for a greater recognition of the support needs of families bereaved by homicide and proposed new legislation which would allow them to be treated with dignity and respect during court proceedings; to avail of the right to information from the Crown Prosecution Service (CPS) and to meet with the CPS lawyer at key stages of the legal process, including on convictions, acquittal or appeal; to avail of sentencing remarks from judges in writing and trial transcripts at a minimal cost to families; to request the release of a body by the coroner back to a family for burial within 28 days unless exceptional circumstances apply; and to be provided with an integrated package of help and support following the death and up until any trial and beyond (Casey, 2011).

Before she had time to implement many of these recommendations, however, a new opportunity arose which led to Casey resigning as Victims' Commissioner. She had previously been an advisor to New Labour on ASB and head of their Respect Task Force, so it was little surprise when, following the English riots in the summer of 2011, she took up a new position as Director General of the Troubled Families Unit. Since then, little has materialized of Casey's endeavours as Victims' Commissioner, with no indication to suggest this work has been (or is intending to be) continued by her replacement, demonstrating issues concerning the continuity of victims' policy.

In December 2012, Baroness Helen Newlove was appointed Victims' Commissioner despite Sara Payne having expressed an interest in the role (BBC News, 2011). Like Payne, Baroness Newlove is another recognizable name due to her media and campaigning work since the murder of her husband Garry in 2007 following an altercation with a group of alcohol-intoxicated young people he suspected had vandalized his wife's car. Much of her awareness-raising since then has been focused on ASB and irresponsible drinking, leading to her previous incarnation as the government's Champion for Active Safer Communities, where she worked with local people to make communities safer and to find solutions for local problems. Her remit as the current Victims' Commissioner, however, is less clear; despite being in post for over a year, the Ministry of Justice website details a single press release from August 2013 and six speeches which have been delivered since December 2012. The only projected output for the remainder of Baroness Newlove's three-year tenure is a report to be produced by the end of 2014 on the delivery of the newest incarnation of the Victims' Code, assessing whether victims have achieved the redress promised if the Code is breached, and whether a victim's right to read their statements personally in court is being delivered in practice.

It is notable that the roles of both the Victims' Champion and the Victims' Commissioner have been allocated to women; two of which were also indirect victims of crime through bereavement. Women are in a minority with regards to being victims of crime, unless this victimization comprises domestic or sexual abuse. Trends in crime and victimization repeatedly indicate that *men* are most likely to be both the perpetrator *and* the victim in criminal offences. Enlisting women with strong social (and media) *capital* but without much real statutory *power* as victims' figurehead suggests a political 'feminizing' of victimization. In addition, this may also be evidence of gendered tokenism in an otherwise masculine-dominated criminal justice system.

The Victims' Minister

The work of the Victims' Commissioner has been coupled with a selection of victim-focused ministerial roles established by the Coalition, each slightly different in scope but each related to the appointment of a 'Victims' Minister', usually affiliated to another ministerial role held at the time. The position has a fairly broad remit, encompassing 'victims, victim support services and sponsorship of the CICA' (HM Government, 2013a). However the position has been characterized by instability, with four ministers holding this portfolio in less than three years. Furthermore, three of the four ministers held the position of Parliamentary Under-Secretary of State at the time, a role characterized as being the lowest of three ministerial tiers, junior to both a Minister of State and a Secretary of State.

The first Victims' Minister was Jonathan Djanogly, MP for Huntingdon, appointed Minister for Victims and the Courts in 2010. Part of his duties as Parliamentary Under-Secretary at the Ministry of Justice involved presiding over the passage of the Legal Aid, Sentencing and Punishment of Offenders Act (2012). The Act is wide-ranging, but includes the establishment of the Legal Aid Agency which replaced the Legal Services Commission. Aside from swingeing cuts to legal aid, the headline problems with the Act relate to the evidence required by victims of domestic violence wishing to access such support. To be entitled to legal aid, victims of domestic violence must provide 'trigger evidence' which proves that they are a victim of abuse. The Ministry of Justice

DOI: 10.1057/9781137409270.0009

website contains a list of acceptable evidence, which includes criminal convictions, a police caution, an undertaking, a letter from a domestic violence refuge and so forth. The website also provides template letters which victims can complete to request confirmation of their victim status. Obtaining the relevant evidence can be expensive with a doctor's letter costing about £50, a memorandum of conviction £60 and a police disclosure £75. Women who are seeking asylum and have no recourse to public funds face even greater hardship in being able to meet these costs. This policy appears to jar with the government's desired 'victim-focused' agenda, aligning instead with their focus on austerity and cuts to public services.

In 2012, Helen Grant, MP for Maidstone and the Weald, took over as Victims' Minister. Being female and from a minority ethnic background, Grant illustrated the Conservative's efforts to become more representative of the electorate by increasing the number of women and ethnic minority MPs from 17 and 9 to 49 and 11 respectively (Ashe et al., 2010). Grant's role as Victim's Minister was held simultaneously to her other responsibilities as Parliamentary Under-Secretary of State for Justice, and for Women and Equalities. The move to affiliate the Victims' Minister with the Women and Equalities role would initially appear to reinforce the above argument relating to the 'feminization' of victim-focused roles, had it not changed hands again. Grant only held the post for a short period of time before being replaced by Shailesh Vara in ministerial re-shuffle in October 2013. Vara, who succeeded Djanogly in 2012 as Parliamentary Under-Secretary of State for the Ministry of Justice with responsibility for the Courts and Legal Aid, barely had time to settle into the role of Victims' Minister before it was passed on again.

Without fanfare or announcement, Damian Green, MP for Ashford, was appointed to the newly titled role of Minister of State for Policing, Criminal Justice and Victims. This is potentially headline news, with victims' needs being promoted to a full ministerial role. However, when perusing the HM Government to understand Green's remit a little better, his detailed list of 28 responsibilities (at the time of writing) unusually fails to mention the word 'victim' once. Nonetheless, a current policy being developed is *Helping and Supporting Victims of Crime*, which recognizes that 'despite improvements over the last 2 decades, the system has continued to fall short in helping victims recover from crime, supporting them through the stresses of investigation and trial, and providing the right support at the right time' (HM Government, 2014). As a result, the

DOI: 10.1057/9781137409270.0009

policy aims to improve support services, particularly for those who need it most (such as victims of serious crime, vulnerable and intimidated victims, and repeat victims) through the commissioning of victims' services both nationally and locally using money claimed from offenders as part of an increased move towards offender responsibilization. This latter aspect relates to the Victim Surcharge, an initiative which compels offenders to financially support victims through enhanced 'fines' which are subsequently channelled into local victims' organizations. The objective is to increase the financial resources available to victims' services by an extra £50 million annually (in addition to the £66 million annually provided to victims' services by central government).

Damien Green's most notable victim-focused initiative to date has also been within this particular policy: pledging £500,000 to support male victims of rape and sexual violence, the first such dedicated fund of its kind. In an announcement on his ministerial site, Green claimed that 'around twelve per cent of rapes are against men', citing police recorded figures of 2,164 rape and sexual assaults against males aged 13 and above in the year ending September 2013. However, he cautioned that this may be an under-estimation as many victims choose not to come forward to report the crime or seek support. According to the Crime Survey for England and Wales, an estimated 72,000 males experience sexual offences annually (Ministry of Justice, 2013). Despite recognizing that average sentences for male rape have increased, the announcement also indicated the government's plan to 'toughen up sentencing' through the introduction of a mandatory life sentence for anyone convicted of a second very serious sexual or violent crime. The move to take male victims of sexual violence seriously is to be welcomed, but poses questions regarding the politicization of victims: namely, whether there is a gendered dynamic to this most recent pledge (by a male minister to male victims) and whether similar promises of financial support will feature following the 2015 general election.

The baton-passing approach to the Victims' Minister position also demonstrates the constantly changing nature of the priority the government ascribed to victims of crime. The Coalition (at the time of writing) holds two statutory figureheads in the Victims' Minister and Victims' Commissioner. Although both are victim-focused, the agendas for each role are incredibly difficult to locate and there is very little evidence to show they are working together, or with the new Police and Crime

DOI: 10.1057/9781137409270.0009

Commissioners, who are specifically tasked with overseeing victim services in their constituency.

Police and Crime Commissioners

The role of Police and Crime Commissioner constitutes another Coalition-created victim figurehead. The reform of Police Authorities as part of a wider commitment to increased police accountability was mirrored in both the Conservative and Liberal Democrat manifestos in the run-up to the 2010 general election. The ensuing Coalition Agreement established the role of a directly elected individual responsible for overseeing the work of the police (HM Government, 2010). Selected at force level, PCCs are tasked to 'hold Chief Constables and their forces to account, effectively making the police answerable to the communities they serve' (Home Office, 2011a: 1). These individuals replace Police Authorities as directed by the Police Reform and Social Responsibility Act 2011. Any resident of the police force area can stand for election, providing they are over eighteen; a British, Commonwealth or EU citizen; not a public servant and have not been convicted of an imprisonable crime. Overall, these officials represent a more publically accountable figurehead than the Victims' Champion or indeed the Victims' Commissioner.

The first PCC elections were held in November 2012 and a large proportion of candidates' campaigning contained a heavy victim-focused rhetoric. For example, Victim Support ran a high-profile campaign asking candidates to sign up to 'Five Promises' for victims and witnesses: to be open and accountable to victims and witnesses, seeking out and acting on their views; to ensure that victims and witnesses get the high quality help and support they need, when they need it; to make the police more victim-focused and more effective at meeting their needs; to give victims and witnesses an effective voice in the wider criminal justice system; and to constantly work to develop new ways of delivering justice for victims.

Over a 100 prospective PCCs signed up to these Promises; upon election, 32 of the 41 PCCs were identifiable as signatories to the campaign (Victim Support Website, 2012).

At first glance, this appears to be a positive step for victims in terms of visibility, accountability and tangible outcomes. However, when translated into practice it seems that some PCCs have delegated victims' work to their deputies, or instigated their own local Victims' Champions

DOI: 10.1057/9781137409270.0009

and Commissioners. With 36 of the 42 democratically elected PCCs being male, in cases where the victims' role or responsibility has been specifically demarcated to a subordinate female, further indications that victimization is being feminized appear evident. In addition, this step to appoint a subordinate to deal with victims appears to be a re-interpretation of Victims' Minister Damian Green's request in a speech he made on the first anniversary of the election of nationwide PCCs where he stated: 'I want to see PCCs become victims' champions at a local level in every force area' (HM Government, 2013a). Competition between local Victims' Champions may be further enhanced by the need to source funding and manage service provision.

In February 2014, Damian Green MP announced that a new £12 million fund was open to PCCs for the provision of support to victims of the most serious crimes, supplementary to their yearly budget (HM Government, 2014a). From October 2014, PCCs will therefore be respon-sible for commissioning the majority of local victims' services (with the exception of support for very serious crimes such as trafficking, which will retain a national funding framework). The intention is for PCCs to source local services provided by voluntary, community and social enterprise organizations through competitive commissioning. This is the result of the 'Getting it Right for Victims and Witnesses' consultation, which is going ahead despite the government's acknowledgement of the criticisms regarding the commissioning out of services which this proposal received from stakeholders at the consultation stage (Ministry of Justice, 2012). At best, this could translate into locally driven respon-sive victim-led policies; at worst, there could be piecemeal provision dependent on the individual PCC's priorities and perceptions of need. This could then lead to a postcode style lottery of inconsistent support available to victims dependent upon which police force area they reside in and which crime(s) they have experienced.

Despite the broad eligibility criteria, the majority of elected PCCs were politically affiliated, indicating a need to be alert for the potential politici-zation of their policies. Of the 43 forces, 31 PCCs have a party allegiance: 13 to Labour, 17 to the Conservatives (including Boris Johnson as Mayor of London for the Metropolitan Police), 1 to the Liberal Democrats, and 11 to independents, with the City of London being overseen by the City of London Corporation. Gilmore (2012) reports how the strongest findings from polls conducted by YouGov and RUSI reflect heightened public concern over the politicization of the police. It is likely that such

DOI: 10.1057/9781137409270.0009

concerns may be transferred to PCCs. Politicization could impact on the equitable provision of local victims' services if decisions are led by nationally driven political ideology towards certain victims at the expense of others. This issue sits alongside broader concerns about the public's understanding of the PCC role (Edwards, 2012), in addition to structural issues raised by the Independent Police Commission (2013) relating to elections and turnout, composition, invisibility, appointment of staff, relationships between the PCCs and Chief Constables and scope of the size of constituency. Additional research conducted by YouGov and Victim Support ahead of the 2012 PCC elections suggested that despite many candidates' vociferously victim-focused campaigning, less than a quarter of the people they surveyed (23%) believed that victims would be a priority for PCCs in practice, with just one in five (18%) believing that PCCs would make a positive difference to the support victims received (YouGov, 2012). This is interesting given that such a heavy focus on victim rhetoric was evident in PCC election campaigns, thus indicating that PCC candidates thought on some level that they were tapping into the core issues that resonated with their electorate. In practice, it may not matter that people believe PCCs to be ineffective for victims, but it may mean that PCCs try harder to address community issues as a result of such survey findings.

Accountability is a more pressing issue, however. Despite being much-maligned and enacted to hold *Chief Constables* accountable, PCCs also offer a convenient mechanism for the Coalition to diffuse their *own* responsibility for victims' services. With the enactment of PCCs as localized figureheads, should anything go wrong with policies or their implementation then it is the PCC who will normally be held accountable. Depending on the seriousness of the issue in hand, this could result in the elected representative ultimately being removed from post. Whether the accountability will travel any higher up the political chain is, at this point, unlikely.

As has been illustrated in this section, victims have never known such socio-political representation with various victims' figureheads currently in existence. However, whilst they all share a victim-focused remit, the level to which these roles work together (if at all) to achieve their aims is questionable. Indeed, each role is an additional layer of bureaucracy and further evidence of the degree to which victimization is becoming subject to administrative processes. These processes allude to the concepts of governmentality and displaced governance discussed in Chapter 1.

DOI: 10.1057/9781137409270.0009

There are numerous conceptual frameworks which would account for a state's recourse to invoking processes which lead to an enhanced level of administration within a victim paradigm. The present analysis suggests that the need to portray control and authority whilst at the same time putting in place buffers to lessen direct accountability may be one reason why so many new victim-focused roles have been established in the past decade. Deflecting attention from the main source of power to subordinate representatives offers a level of distance. Other factors informing the state's increasing trend towards more administration and less accountability may be linked to the contemporary socio-political climate. In order to explore this in more depth the following section examines the context within which increased mechanisms of victim bureaucracy have emerged. In doing so, it questions the advantages that such mechanisms offer the Coalition to deflect attention away from its inability to *prevent* victimization, and instead appear to retain legitimacy through its *management* of victimization.

Deviance, austerity and social change

The following section outlines several events which have occurred during the Coalition's reign which have impacted on the social constructions of victimization and the tolerance towards deviance. The dynamic process of deviancy creation has been extensively debated elsewhere in theoretical terms; thus there is no intention to cover old ground (see Elias, 1994). The focus here is on real-life events, specifically since New Labour came to power in 1997, given that there have been significant social changes which have likely influenced how both the public and CJS comprehend and consider deviance in contemporary society. The reputation of politics, and of several politicians, in the UK was significantly damaged by the 'MPs expenses scandal' of 2011. As will be demonstrated, when 'society' (aka, the taxpayer) is the victim of ministerial economic deviance, the juxtaposition with aforementioned typologies is rendered problematic as the 'offender' is part of the same group tasked with punishing deviance whilst deflecting attention away to 'real' victims.

Similarly, advances in social media and networking technologies have allowed greater levels of deviance to proliferate through society and create victims (often anonymously) and have further blurred the lines between victims and offenders. In light of these factors, the categorizing

DOI: 10.1057/9781137409270.0009

of discernable victims and perpetrators of criminal offences which can be typified and logged according to crime or victim type is advantageous to a government which would rather the public focus instead on *those* sorts of criminals. The focus here informs a later analysis concerning the degree to which an enhanced promotion of victim policy proves a strategically useful deflection, or political diversion, from 'in-house' problems.

Political economics in an age of austerity

A number of events have strained relations between the public and politicians, which are likely to have influenced not only the mood of the UK, but how deviance is conceptualized. To cut a long story (very) short, the 2008 global economic crisis triggered financial chaos in the UK. This resulted in the government having to 'bail out' some high street banks to the sum of £500 billion, with the part-nationalization of Northern Rock and the Royal Bank of Scotland making headline news. Economies slowed worldwide and from 2008 to 2009, the UK entered the deepest period of recession since World War Two. To counteract this, when they came to power in 2010, the Coalition embarked on the most severe budget cuts of any advanced economy facing pressure to reduce financial deficits (*Financial Times*, 2010). However, despite turbulent economic times and the necessity of bank bail-outs that have been partly attributed to banker greed and risk-taking, bankers' bonuses remained at pre-crash six-figure sums, even in banks with the state as the majority shareholder. This occurred despite initial New Labour government efforts to tax bankers' bonuses by introducing a one-off 50 per cent bank levy on discretionary bonuses over £25,000 in 2010 (HM Treasury, 2009).

Despite the admission from the (then) Chancellor of the Exchequer, Alistair Darling, that the levy failed to alter banking sector attitudes to pay (Wilson, 2010), little headway has since been made in challenging the bonus culture. More recently in September 2013, Coalition Chancellor George Osborne filed a case with the European Court of Justice against an EU-wide cap on bankers' bonuses, claiming it will negatively influence financial stability (*Financial Times*, 2013). The retention of bankers' bonuses for those implicated in the financial crisis, as well as the ensuing austerity measures, has created much public disdain towards the profession. Although capitalism itself can be seen as having an inbuilt tendency for periods of boom and bust, the role several financiers were

DOI: 10.1057/9781137409270.0009

seen to have in the economic crisis was picked up on in the popular press, epitomized by the front-page headlines such as *The Sun* calling the bankers 'Scumbag Millionaires' (*The Sun*, 2009). For many, an 'us' and 'them' dichotomy developed along socio-economic lines, with 'deviant' bankers both blamed and seen to be allowed to 'get-away' with causing a tremendous amount of turmoil. The focus on individuals, rather than wider circumstances, also conveniently deflected attention away from the problematic structural underpinnings of capitalism and neoliberal ideology and on to the modern day 'folk devils' of the economic crisis.

This dichotomy has been compounded by the MPs' parliamentary expenses scandal, where actual and speculated misuse of permitted expenses, totalling hundreds of thousands of pounds, was exposed by the *Daily Telegraph* in 2009. In the months that followed, the MPs involved took a variety of actions including public apologies, repaying their claims (totalling £1.46 million (BBC News, 2011)), announcing their retirement, with some also being sacked. Five MPs have served prison sentences following criminal charges of false accounting. It was the nature of the illegitimate claims that really focused the publics' wrath, with items such as a £1645 floating duck house (Sir Peter Viggers), £380 worth of horse manure (David Heathcoat-Amory), and at the other end of the scale, eight pence was claimed for a 0.2 mile car journey (Ed Vaizey). These examples further emphasize the distinction between those financially blasé with the public purse and the broader general public. As the public's perceptions towards those in positions of financial responsibility deteriorated, contemporary conceptualizations of deviance and deviant behaviour were formed.

This new public outrage was, and still is at the time of writing, set within the context of austerity, which plays a key role in many of the arguments put forward in this book. To clarify the extent of the situation, the first spending reductions announced in the Spending Review (October, 2010) indicated real terms cuts to the Home Office budget of 27 per cent, with Ministry of Justice funds being cut by 23 per cent (HM Treasury, 2010). In the most recent Spending Round (June 2013), a further £11.5 billion was required to be saved, with the Home Office and Ministry of Justice facing further overall budget reductions of 4.6 per cent and 7 per cent respectively (HM Treasury, 2013). The impact in reality is demonstrated by the assertion that police strength is currently at its lowest level since 2002 (House of Commons Library, 2013) and that

DOI: 10.1057/9781137409270.0009

cuts to crime prevention budgets have totalled over £35 million since 2010 (Morris, 2012).

Austerity measures have not only affected the CJS; £18 billion has been cut from welfare budgets between 2010 and 2014/15, and a further £3.6 billion of cuts has been scheduled for the end of parliament in 2015 (HM Treasury, 2013). Examples of welfare austerity impacting upon the most vulnerable members of society include changes to housing benefit through the Welfare Reform Act 2012. The most high-profile of these changes is known colloquially as the Bedroom Tax. This restricts housing benefit in the social rented sector by allowing one bedroom per person or couple (with a few exceptions relating to sharing rules for siblings of different genders, those serving in the Armed Forces, foster carers and non-resident overnight carers). For those tenants with a 'spare' room, housing benefit is cut at a fixed rate of 14 per cent for one extra room and 25 per cent for two extra rooms, with 600,000 tenants projected to be affected (National Housing Federation, 2014). According to initial figures released in November 2013, 522,000 people have faced reductions in housing benefit as a result (Wintour, 2013).

The context of austerity and the negative impact it has had on the poorest people in society adds an extra layer of resentment towards the bankers and politicians. Therefore, subtle shifts in victim policy to refocus on 'real' victims of 'criminally deviant' conduct may prove advantageous in going some way to redress this sentiment. However, simultaneous to anti-banker and politician sentiment, public attitudes towards welfare have hardened, with the public now more likely to suggest individual factors are the cause of poverty than societal ones (NatCen Social Research, 2014). This attitude contrasts the views previously held during times of recession (Joseph Rowntree Foundation, 2014), which reaffirms a broader shift in public opinion, which may reflect the return to neoliberal, law and order policies espoused by the Coalition.

Twitter, trolling and tolerance

Another key element of social change that must be addressed and which strongly relates to conceptions of deviance is the advent and proliferation of social media. Essentially the term 'social media' applies to the interactions of people in virtual spaces, with Facebook, Instagram and Twitter being popular forums. Since its creation in 2006, Twitter in particular has become an immensely prevalent means of sharing information. Twitter

DOI: 10.1057/9781137409270.0009

accounts promulgated by news agencies, criminal justice stakeholders and campaigners alike have increased the accessibility of crime and victim news. Furthermore, the medium has developed into a platform used to campaign for change with accounts such as the *Everyday Sexism Project*, which documents experiences of sexism, harassment and assault to increase the visibility of these problems, having over 100,000 'followers' worldwide (Everyday Sexism Project, 2014). However, the rise in popularity of social media has not been without its problems, the details of which can be examined through the twin lenses of 'defining deviancy up' (Krauthammer, 1993) and 'defining deviancy down' (Moynihan, 1993), in order to make sense of how social media has affected contemporary conceptions of deviance.

Krauthammer (1993: 20) suggests 'as part of the vast social project of moral levelling, it is not enough for the deviant to be normalized. The normal must be found to be deviant'. He claims ordinary people are increasingly guilty of new forms of deviance in comparison to traditionally deviant criminal behaviours, which are increasingly seen as normal. Twitter has unleashed a vast grey area surrounding the limits of free speech, where individuals have been taken to court for making inappropriate jokes or distasteful and offensive comments. For example, Paul Chambers was convicted (but eventually cleared) of jokingly tweeting about the closure of an airport due to snow: 'Crap! Robin Hood airport is closed. You've got a week and a bit to get your shit together otherwise I'm blowing the airport sky high!!' (Bowcott, 2012). At the more severe end of the social media scale, the way in which some people use Twitter has created a new type of victimization known as Twitter 'trolling'. This is where individuals abuse and harass others, usually under unidentifiable handles and user names. High-profile cases have included Cambridge Professor Mary Beard receiving a bomb threat following a television appearance and feminist campaigner Caroline Criado-Perez receiving threats of rape and murder after campaigning for women to be represented on bank notes (Kennedy, 2013). Two of Criado-Perez's abusers were found guilty under section 127(1) (A) of the Communications Act 2003; Isabella Sorley was jailed for 12 weeks and co-defendant John Nimmo was jailed for eight weeks. Consequently there is a case to be made for the threshold of unacceptable speech having been defined up to include the inappropriate and distasteful, resulting in additional types of behaviour considered to be 'bad'. Some of the victim-led policies which will be explored in relation to ASB relate to a similar process of defining

DOI: 10.1057/9781137409270.0009

deviancy up, particularly in relation to Injunctions to Prevent Nuisance and Annoyance.

In contrast, as Moynihan (1993) contends, certain types of behaviour can become normalized and almost expected. Although prosecutions ensued in the Criado-Perez case, numerous incidents of racist and homophobic abuse posted on Twitter go unchallenged, unreported and unsanctioned. This is illustrated by the homophobic abuse received by Tom Daley after he announced on YouTube that he was in a relationship with a man (Storify, 2013). Consequently the pervasiveness and tolerance towards *certain* types of online abuse appears to have been normalized. Therefore what we are faced with in 2014 is a heady mix of tolerable and intolerable behaviours, some of which are very similar, but all do not attract criminal sanction.

More recent examinations of tolerance contribute to the emergence of the politicized victim by highlighting the subjectivity of some types of victimization. Tolerance is intimately linked to the notion of subjectivity, which relates to the perception of deviance and is governed by factors such as context, location, community tolerance and quality of life expectations (Nixon et al., 2003). Bannister and Kearns (2009: 182) suggest 'the sociospatial situation in which we find ourselves both influences our predisposition towards tolerance and determines a set of other drivers of the tolerant response, so that our thresholds of tolerance are spatially specific and spatially variant'. Consequently, some types of behaviour may be accepted in an urban setting but not in a neighbourhood setting. Therefore levels of tolerance and behavioural expectations may fuel or lessen perceptions of victimization. Supplementary to these ideas is the influence government policy may have upon tolerance levels. By creating sanctions to respond to these behaviours, tolerance levels are likely to decrease further by eliminating opportunities to interact with others that can build common trust and values (Bannister and Kearns, 2009). This demonstrates how tolerance and subjectivity can be used politically to demarcate and prioritize certain types of victims.

To summarize, the examples outlined in the above section demonstrate how increases in the politicization and administration of victimization are set in the context of a seemingly disgruntled and cash-strapped UK, where behavioural tolerance is being constantly redefined. Victims have played a key role in criminal justice and social discourses as and when it has suited a political, scholarly or electoral agenda, but their independent 'voice' appears muted. The following chapter takes the two policy

DOI: 10.1057/9781137409270.0009

domains of ASB and hate crime and applies a case-study approach to the most recent political and legislative developments related to these arenas. In doing so, the analysis explores how victims have been used by policy makers to administer an enhanced and retributive process of crime and deviancy control which may be 'victim-focused' but remains *responsive*, as opposed to *preventative*, in scope.

Summary of key points

- ▶ The Coalition government has undergone some turbulent times since its inception in 2010, with questions raised concerning its legitimacy and mandate.
- ▶ Changes to the victims sector have arisen as a result of ongoing processes associated with a neoliberal agenda.
- ▶ Several figureheads have been established and tasked with providing victims with a greater level of visibility in the criminal justice system.
- ▶ Austerity policies and developments in social media have altered both the mood and behavioural tolerance levels of the public.

Note

1 Following the exposure of television personality Jimmy Savile as a prolific sexual offender, calls to women's organizations, rape crisis centres and the police by victims of sexual assault increased dramatically as people began to feel more able to speak about what happened to them.

DOI: 10.1057/9781137409270.0009

3
Prioritized Political Focus: ASB and Hate Crime

Abstract: *Chapter 3 adopts a prioritized focus on ASB and hate crime policy to investigate* contemporary *policy developments in light of the 'victim-focused' rhetoric espoused by the Coalition government. A critical overview of political interventions in these areas illustrates how* right-realist *ideology is informing enhanced criminalization or control under the guise of being* victim-focused. *The near-farcical fluctuation in political responses to ASB has been echoed by the conveyer-belt approach to defining acronyms designed to be synonymous with this particular Coalition government, whilst recent proposals to enhance and extend hate crime sanctions indicate that policy approaches remain responsive, as opposed to preventative, in this domain.*

Keywords: ASB; community sanctions; deviancy; enhanced punishment; hate crime

Duggan, Marian and Vicky Heap. *Administrating Victimization: The Politics of Anti-Social Behaviour and Hate Crime Policy.* Basingstoke: Palgrave Macmillan, 2014. DOI: 10.1057/9781137409270.0010.

Several subtle shifts with regards to prioritizing groups, or types, of victims in the criminal justice system have been taking place since the mid-1990s. Drawing on the meta-themes of socio-political developments in victim visibility, the return towards categorization along the basis of victim identity or experience, and what the Coalition's 'putting victims first' rhetoric looks like in practice, this chapter focuses on *contemporary* changes within victim policy in two specific domains: anti-social behaviour (ASB) and hate crime. These areas of victimization may also involve some level of interpersonal interaction between victim(s) and perpetrator(s) which may be closely linked in nature, scope and impact. However, according to whether the act is deemed ASB or hate crime, the construction of, and responses to, the victim(s) and the perpetrator(s) are notably different due to separate interventions and procedures.

As ASB policy has been re-branded by the Coalition as *victim*-focused, an opposing strategy to New Labour's agenda which focused primarily on *offenders*, legislation has introduced new powers for victims to hold authorities to account. The ASB, Crime and Policing Act (2014) streamlines existing ASB legislation and, whilst there are indications of continuity here with New Labour's agenda, further punitive sanctions can be seen as an attempt to attract voters. Similarly, with regards to hate crime, the Law Commission has recently closed consultations (held at the behest of the government) which addressed proposals to extend existing penalties for hate crime offences. This would enhance punishments for offences which are motivated by disability, sexual orientation or gender identity hostility, equalizing them with existing 'aggravated' categories which currently pertain to race and religion.

From a political and crime prevention perspective, the segregating and individualizing of these types of victimization indicate further problems. As will be outlined in the following section, for ASB these proposals refocus some of the responsibility for safety and vigilance on the victim (past, present or potential). Similarly, for hate crime the focus on enhanced or expanded criminalization and criminal justice interventions which *respond* to rather than *prevent* victimization is of little use to many victims, nor does it address the high volume of lower-level, everyday incidents which constitute forms of micro-victimization seen to be too minor and/or frequent to continually report. These enhancement proposals also require that hate crime victims – whose previously criminalized identities now constitute sites of vulnerability – actively engage with the CJS in a co-operative and collaborative manner to avail of the type of justice promoted. In sum, focusing on criminal justice-inspired responsive measures absolves the state from confronting its social, political, economic, welfare and education responsibilities to address problems which may result in targeted interpersonal victimization occurring in the first place.

Focus on: anti-social behaviour

ASB is synonymous with New Labour following their introduction of a broad range of legislative tools and powers to tackle nuisance and disorderly behaviour. However, they were not the first political party to legislate against nuisance, with previous Conservative governments laying the foundations to sanction disorderly conduct through the Public Order Act (1986), which without explicitly using the term ASB, introduced the power to sanction many behaviours that are considered anti-social today. The Housing Act (1996) was also pivotal, for as Flint (2006) contends, much ASB policy has been generated from a housing context, thus housing – specifically issues surrounding tenure – have remained at the forefront of ASB debates.

Origins and developments

The seminal policy associated with New Labour's redefinition of nuisance is the anti-social behaviour order (hereafter referred to as ASBO). The Crime and Disorder Act (1998) has enabled authorities to apply for ASBOs since 1999, to prevent behaviour that 'causes or is likely to cause harassment, alarm or distress'. The civil orders were administered by the Magistrates' Court and given to anyone over the age of ten. ASBOs operated for a minimum of two years, with no restriction on the type(s) of behaviour they sanctioned or how many prohibitive conditions the order contained. There were four general types of ASBO conditions: geographical, restricting where the recipient can go; temporal, restricting the times the recipient can be in certain places; association, restricting who the recipient can meet; and behavioural, restricting certain types of behaviour.

The ability to sanction these behaviours extended powers of the Housing Act (1996), which only sanctions the nuisance behaviour of

DOI: 10.1057/9781137409270.0010

council and social housing tenants. There is nothing in statute to prevent an order being given for a single act of ASB, but local councils and ASB Units often ask victims to record an incident diary, where a pattern of persistent ASB can be identified, following Home Office Guidance (Home Office, 1999). The behaviours sanctioned against do not have to be criminal acts, but criminal behaviour such as graffiti (criminal damage) can be prohibited by an ASBO. The reasonableness and circumstances of the alleged ASB are taken into consideration by the court (Crime and Disorder Act 1998, section 1 (5)), therefore behaviour causing only minor harassment, alarm or distress may be dismissed. However, the court has no duty to consider the reasonableness of the reaction to the behaviour, which in some cases may be disproportionate to the behaviour itself, given that the subjective nature of tolerance in respect of ASB is a very individual matter. What one person considers reasonable may constitute ASB for another. A disproportionate reaction towards the behaviour may be a consequence of the all-encompassing definition of ASB, taking into consideration the vast amount of behaviours that could cause harassment, alarm or distress to the victim. Moreover, there is no legal stipulation that the acts causing harassment, alarm or distress are conducted intentionally. Therefore thoughtless behaviour affords the same sanctions as malicious, targeted ASB. This relates to earlier discussions in the previous chapter about tolerance levels, as well as other offence categories where subjectivity influences the perception of behaviour such as hate crime (discussed below).

The period between the introduction of ASBOs in 1999 and the Coalition coming to power in 2010 has been turbulent for ASB policy. The domain has witnessed shifts in emphasis, which can be traced to Labour's terms in office. For example, the first term (1997–2001) was characterized by the original emphasis for the ASB agenda, namely nuisance neighbours. This was followed by greater cross-departmental coordination in the second term (2001–2005), with a focus on environmental aspects linked to the use of public space, including sanctions such as Dispersal Orders for young people, as well as fly-posting and graffiti. The third term, from 2005 onwards, was labelled as the era of 'Respect'. The Respect Action Plan (2006) emphasized a dual approach between intervention and enforcement, with key measures including providing constructive and purposeful activities for young people; improving behaviour and attendance in schools; supporting families through addressing poor parenting; taking a new approach with the

DOI: 10.1057/9781137409270.0010

most problematic families including greater persistence of action and joined up working; strengthening communities by giving the public a greater sense of ownership; and creating effective enforcement tools and community justice (Respect Task Force, 2006). Further changes to ASB ensued following the change of Labour leadership from Tony Blair to Gordon Brown in 2007, where the focus centred on young people through a combination of enforcement, support and prevention. The whole Respect agenda was swiftly transformed into the Youth Taskforce and relocated in the newly created Department for Children, School and Families. From 2008 onwards the priority of ASB then appeared to reduce, with no new policies announced prior to the 2010 general election.

Despite the continuous reinventions of the ASB agenda, the vast range of tools and powers were perceived to have little impact. As there has never been a formal evaluation of the effectiveness of powers such as ASBOs, *perceptions* of their efficacy is all that can be measured. ASBOs were hugely maligned, and their use started to decline in 2005, with 58 per cent being breached at least once (this figure relates to only *recorded* breaches) (HM Government, 2013). The challenge for the Coalition, therefore, was to seize the initiative on ASB, in order to tame what had become an unwieldy raft of powers, tools, toolkits and taskforces. After her appointment as Home Secretary, Theresa May marked her intentions as early as July 2010, to 'move beyond the ASBO' (May, 2010). However, after a period of relative silence on ASB as a whole, it was not until the publication of the White Paper *Putting Victims First – More Effective Responses to Anti-Social Behaviour* that victim rhetoric was first introduced to this policy domain. There has been a marked lack of victim focus in academic (or any) accounts of ASB, thus little is known about the true impact of ASB on victims' quality of life or the effectiveness of sanctions or statutory support systems. The overriding focus has tended to be on those receiving ASB sanctions, casting the recipients as victims of a repressive and unjust policy towards marginalized groups, reflecting the punitiveness of the legislation enacted by New Labour. Consequently the shift in emphasis proposed by May was filled with promise. Fundamentally, the Coalition made a commitment '*to ensure that all agencies and individuals focus on the need of victims*' (Home Office, 2012: 17, original emphasis).

Prior to a victim focus entering the equation, much was made of streamlining the number of tools and powers available to practitioners

DOI: 10.1057/9781137409270.0010

to sanction ASB. Six new powers are contained in the ASB, Crime and Policing Act (2014), to make sanctions quicker and easier to obtain. When the Bill progressed through parliament widespread interest was provoked by Part 1, originally entitled 'Injunctions to Prevent Nuisance and Annoyance' (IPNAs). This has resulted in various amendments to the originally intended powers; as such these arguments will be documented to demonstrate Coalition concessions in this area and the potential impact this will have on victims. As a consequence of the amendments Part 1 is due to be renamed, although this has not yet taken place at the time of writing. Therefore the powers contained in this part of Act will be referred to as IPNAs in lieu of their new branding. Overall, the ASB, Crime and Policing Act is too wide-ranging to be covered in full, therefore the three most relevant policies to the politics of victimization will be discussed in the remainder of this section, namely: Part 1, Criminal Behaviour Orders (CBOs or as they are referred to here, CrimBOs) and the Community Trigger.

From ASBOs to IPNAs (to IPASBs?)

IPNAs were the headline-grabbing, all-encompassing ASBO replacement that originally constituted Part 1 of the Bill. The rationale for these measures was to prevent low-level ASB quickly and easily before it escalates. IPNAs are essentially modelled on ASBIs (anti-social behaviour injunctions), which were only available to social landlords, and found by Heap (2010) to be a popular sanction for 'nipping problems in the bud'. Indeed, perhaps reflecting the housing-related context of much ASB, findings from Clarke et al. (2011) show how ASBIs were more prevalent in some locations than ASBOs, demonstrating how this type of injunction was already well-established in the social housing sphere.

The original intention for IPNAs was to make them applicable to anyone over the age of ten who 'has engaged or threatens to engage in conduct capable of causing nuisance and annoyance to any person' (Great Britain, Parliament, House of Lords 2013). This was to be coupled with the lower burden of proof, based on the balance of probabilities (which the ASBO started with, until a successful legal challenge). However, these two factors, despite the above definition being in place for the ASBI, have caused great controversy on a number of fronts, with the result generating a dichotomy between those whose priority is to protect victims experiencing ASB and those who seek to defend civil

DOI: 10.1057/9781137409270.0010

liberties and free speech. It was not until the Bill passed to the House of Lords in October 2013 that these contrasting perspectives came to the fore.

Needless to say, the House of Lords appear to be playing for team 'freedoms'. The first amendment they proposed (which was subsequently rejected) was for the Bill to increase the burden of proof to beyond reasonable doubt. This would have aligned IPNAs with existing ASBO provisions, moving it further away from its original roots in the ASBI. The impact of this change would have been potentially damaging to victims of ASB, who are *supposed* to be the focus of these legislative changes. With a higher burden of proof, it is more likely that victims of ASB would be required to give evidence in court, as hearsay and professional witness evidence from police or housing officers alone may not be sufficient to pass the threshold test. ASB victims appearing in court as witnesses can be particularly traumatic, due to the likelihood of the case stemming from a repetitive neighbourhood issue. Heap (2010) found that victims were unlikely to even *report* ASB due to the fear of reprisals, so one can imagine having to potentially give evidence in court for low-level ASB, which IPNAs are supposed to address, would have been a further barrier to reporting. For victims in social housing there is the potential to use alternative sanctions to stop ASB without having to appear as a witness in court; however, the implementation of this approach could have serious consequences for the perpetrators. Social housing groups such as the Social Landlords Crime and Nuisance Group (2013) warn that raising the burden of proof for IPNAs could result in housing providers resorting to Possession Orders to evict anti-social tenants, as possession is obtained via the lower threshold of balance of probabilities. This would lead to homelessness of whole families, which is likely to result in the displacement of the problem rather than a solution. From a victims' perspective, at least this option offers some redress. However, victims in private homes do not benefit from such legislation, potentially creating a hierarchy of ASB victimization.

The Lords did manage to amend one key aspect of the legislation. Perhaps even more disconcertingly for victims, Lord Dear successfully led a vote to block the definition of ASB for IPNAs being based on 'nuisance and annoyance' and return it to the old ASBO definition of 'harassment, alarm or distress'. By aligning the new IPNA with the old ASBI in a definitional sense would have removed the hierarchy of

DOI: 10.1057/9781137409270.0010

victimization witnessed between private and social tenants outlined above and action would be easier to take. This further contradicts the original rationale for IPNAs to quickly address ASB, particularly if private tenant victims cannot utilize other legislation and have to wait until the ASB reaches harassment, alarm or distress proportions before any action can be taken. The proposals for IPNAs to define ASB based on nuisance and annoyance were always going to be contentious; any policy that proposes the quicker and easier disposal of sanctions based on a lower standard of proof is inherently worrying. Therefore despite good intentions on behalf of victims, it appears they are being used here as the method through which to push through a 'law and order' policy.

A survey of the vast amount of ASB literature that debates the legally tighter definition of 'harassment, alarm or distress' highlights the vast array of problems with defining ASB (see Card and Ward, 1998; Bannister and Scott, 2000; Budd and Sims, 2001; and Flint and Nixon, 2006). Lord Dear based his opposition to 'nuisance and annoyance' on concerns of net-widening, risks to fundamental freedoms and free speech, with the potential for certain groups to be unfairly targeted such as carol-singers and nudists. A highly charged debate on the defence of freedoms is best summarized by a quotation from Baroness Mallalieu (HL Debate 2013/14):

> Whoever thought up Clause 1 [definition] and managed to slip it under the radar of the other place is a strong contender for some kind of award. Perhaps it should be a citation for attempting to increase the power of the state to interfere in people's lives; perhaps a golden globe for providing the authorities with a new and easy-to-discharge weapon in the war against inconvenient and annoying expressions of dissent; or perhaps even an Oscar for thinking up a way to take out those who are a nuisance or annoyance in any one of a thousand unspecified ways – and doing it in a manner that admits virtually no defence or safeguard and that requires the minimum of evidence.

Following the success of the amendment, Crime Prevention Minister Norman Baker stated he was 'confident these new powers won't stop people being able to sing carols or whatever else the scare stories say' (*The Guardian*, 2014). However, the Lords and public alike may not feel very confident about these reassurances in practice. Furthermore, the authorities have a track-record for not always using legislation for its intended purpose, such as the deployment of Regulation of Investigatory

Powers Act (2000). This legislation was brought in to prevent terrorism and internet crime, but investigations have found that 26 local authorities have used these surveillance powers to monitor low-level offending, including dog owners to see whose animals were responsible for dog fouling, amongst other things (Big Brother Watch, 2012). To diminish public confidence further still, recent headlines have seen a police officer admitting falsifying his account of an incident involving an MP as part of the 'plebgate scandal' (BBC News, 2014). Also, since the inquest into the fatal police shooting of Mark Duggan returned a conclusion of lawful killing, public trust in the police has been further damaged (Lammy, 2014).

In short, the aforementioned successful amendment to the Bill left IPNAs looking suspiciously similar to the original ASBOs (encompassing the harassment, alarm or distress definition coupled with the lower burden of proof). However, further last-minute amendments fundamentally changed the basis of Part 1, recovering the ASBI origins and splitting IPNAs into two distinct camps: housing and non-housing related ASB. Interestingly these have different definitions of ASB and represent a pivotal change to the new ASB policy, which reinforces the influence and interconnectedness of housing policy and ASB.

Essentially in the first aspect of Part 1 relating to non-housing ASB, IPNAs remain the same as outlined above, retaining their similarities to the very first ASBO legislation. However they will not be called IPNAs due to the removal of the nuisance and annoyance criteria, with a new 'name' for these injunctions expected to be revealed imminently. A mooted option so far has been Injunctions to Prevention ASB, or IPASBs, which is not as neat an acronym, so a return to 'ASBI' is possible. The second element of Part 1 is the real game-changer, as it specifies housing providers, police and local authorities can apply for an injunctions relating to housing-related ASB. It retains the 'nuisance and annoyance' definition, as well as the lower standard of proof. This effectively creates a tenure-neutral ASBI, allowing private tenants and owner-occupiers to access to this commonly used piece of legislation, ameliorating the existing hierarchy between these groups. A greater equity of provision is a marked step forward, however it is likely private households will not have the same level of support in pursuit of these injunctions (at least at the outset) as social tenants, who have vastly experienced housing association professionals to steer the process. Little has been said about the services to be put in place to advocate on behalf of private households, such as who they will report ASB to. As the Act refers to local authorities it appears the burden will fall to them, although whether they will have the resources in place to facilitate cases remains to be seen, in terms of both personnel and financial resources in this era of budget cuts, something which Brown (2013) suggests is already a concern for social housing providers. However, the amendment does provide a greater indication about the types of ASB invoking this sanction. It is likely the public will be able to better recognize ASB as being housing related through an understanding of nuisance neighbours, as opposed to the abstract terms of nuisance and annoyance. In a sense this takes ASB back to its legislative roots in the Housing Act and the original roots of ASB created by New Labour. Consequently it appears ASB has gone full circle and is now looking more like it used to in 1998 than the intervening years.

The key difference between the old and new legislation relates to breach of the injunction and the new 'positive' requirement. The breach proposals have been less overtly controversial, but are deeply concerning for victims and offenders alike. IPNAs are not inherently criminal on breach, like ASBOs, although the court can impose further sanctions on the recipient, for which the criminal standard of proof is required. According to draft Home Office Guidance (2013: 27), in adult cases 'breach is dealt with by a civil contempt of court ... The imprisonment is for the contempt of court, not for the conduct'. The punishment for this is up to two years imprisonment and/or an unlimited fine. For those under 18, matters are dealt with by the Youth Court with the punishment resulting in a Supervision Order or at the severe end of the scale a Detention Order. However, if the punishment is based on breaching the injunction and not for committing the behaviour itself, situating sanctions on a sliding scale proves problematic on two key bases. First, the intricacies of IPNA breach not being criminal, but being punished criminally is confusing for both victims and offenders. It is safe to assume that the average person will not know about the finer detail of civil contempt of court. For the victim who has just seen their perpetrator handed an IPNA, the message received is that breach is not criminal. This further underlines some of the perennial issues ASB sanctions have had with public confidence and trust, thus leading to dubiousness regarding the efficacy of an IPNA. When comparing IPNAs to ASBOs, their efficacy to stopping the act of ASB is questionable. The failure to consider ASBOs effective, even with the threat of criminal proceedings upon breach, does not bode well for IPNAs

DOI: 10.1057/9781137409270.0010

which exist without such an obvious deterrent effect.[1] How safe this will make victims feel when pursuing these sanctions, and how likely is it that the ASB will stop, is also questionable. Much has been made of the potential for positive requirements fixed within IPNAs to support and help change behaviour, but such conditions are not compulsory and there is no evidence to suggest this additional element will prompt the cessation of ASB. So essentially it appears IPNAs will simply be an ASBO with less clout, a toothless tiger that fails to achieve for victims what it promised.

The inclusion of positive requirements has been added to both the IPNA and CrimBO sanctions, although injunctions do not have to contain this positive aspect. It simply legislates that recipients do something to address their behaviour, such as attend anger management sessions or drugs and alcohol treatment. Failure to comply will result in breach in the same way as the traditional prohibitions. The usual provisions have been made in the Act to ensure these requirements are 'reasonable', however this casts the net of sanctioned behaviours even wider, creating the possibility that someone could technically be imprisoned for not complying with something they *should* be doing. This level of contractual governance and social control is unprecedented, taking the criminalization associated with ASBOs (that of breaching conditions that represent non-criminal behaviours) one step further by criminalizing a non-event. These developments affect victims; if the sanctions are not viable, or are unrealistic, they will not produce the intended consequences meaning the suffering incurred by victims of ASB is less likely to subside. This underlines how the Coalition's ASB policy is not truly focused on victims, particularly in regards to IPNAs, which contradicts much of their rationale for change.

From CrASBOs to CrimBOs

Criminal Behaviour Orders replace criminal or post-conviction ASBOs, commonly referred to as CrASBOs. They are available post-conviction for *any* criminal offence and last from a minimum of two years to an indefinite period. These are based on the original 'harassment, alarm or distress' definition, and retain the criminal burden of proof. The new addition to these orders is the positive requirement element to address the causes of ASB. CrASBOs have been typically used to place geographic conditions on convicted shoplifters to 'ban' them from shopping

DOI: 10.1057/9781137409270.0010

precincts, in spite of the threat of spatial displacement. On face value CrimBOs appear favourable to victims. For example, it will allow the court to hand down a CrimBO to an offender convicted of hate crime, to prohibit further instances of hate and require the offender to participate in an activity designed to prevent further hate crime incidents in the future by addressing the causes of hate.

The biggest test will be finding agencies, both statutory and non-statutory, with the capacity to deliver these positive requirements at a time of austerity and budget cuts. The Act states in Part 2, 23(1) that the order must state a person or organization responsible for supervising compliance with the order. In addition in 23(4), that person or organization must promote the offender's compliance. There has to date been no mention of additional funds being made available for agencies to facilitate these positive requirements. Considering pragmatic issues of implementation, by the time the behaviour has escalated to a criminal extent, such provisions may be too late for victims who will have already suffered a threshold of victimization high enough to bring about criminal proceedings. Alternatively, CrimBOs may simply be the next progressive step on the sanction ladder. This is potentially where the proposed changes to IPNAs will have an effect on victims. Without a lower-level order to sanction ASB, a CrimBO might provide the first opportunity for victims to see their perpetrator sanctioned. By re-introducing 'harassment, alarm or distress' and the criminal burden of proof to IPNAs, essentially the old system of ASBO and CrASBO is being recreated, only this time under slightly different names (and with the option for a positive requirement). So the attempt by the Coalition to re-brand ASB policy, to focus on the needs of victims, has effectively made little or no tangible change. If anything, the re-branding of the CrASBO to the CrimBO conflates crime and ASB. There is an awareness of the difficulties the public face in understanding what ASB actually entails (Heap, 2010; HMIC, 2010). Entitling one of the new ASB sanctions to feature the word 'crime' will do little to address that matter.

Perhaps the most interesting insight into Coalition thoughts on CrimBO use relate to the hate crime example provided and the appearance of hate crime within the Home Office draft guidance document for the reformed powers. As Duggan and Heap (2013) contest, ASB and hate crime share a number of connections, however such connections have never been presented in any previous Home Office publications. The

DOI: 10.1057/9781137409270.0010

inclusion now is likely in response to a number of tragic cases where hate crime has been tackled unsuccessfully using ASB powers, the most high profile being the case of Fiona Pilkington, who killed herself and her severely disabled daughter in 2007 following years of harassment by local youths. However, the guidance is merely descriptive of hate crime, stating only that 'incidents of hate crime may manifest themselves in low level forms of anti-social behaviour, which on the surface may appear minor but the impact on the victim and their families may be devastating and life changing' (Home Office, 2013: 9). It does not address or advise how practitioners can help victims, following up this piecemeal offering by stating that responses to hate crime should be enacted at a local level, representing a tokenistic attempt to embrace the needs of hate crime victims.

Further sporadic attempts to integrate ASB and hate crime provision are evidenced in additional Lords' amendments to the Bill, specifically clause 96 (review of response to complaints). More colloquially known as the Community Trigger, this piece of legislation will force relevant bodies to act if victims perceive their reports of ASB to have been ignored. Victims can request a review of their case, with the caveat for a review being the relevant authorities agree a specified threshold has been met. This threshold is to be locally set, but early Home Office literature indicates a threshold of five individual complaints from five different households, or three complaints from an individual about the same issue in the same neighbourhood in the past six months, where no action has been taken (Home Office, 2011). The link to hate crime inserted into clause 96 extends the parameters of a review by stating that a case review should be granted not only if the complainant is a victim of ASB, but also if the victim is 'vulnerable due to ill health, mental capacity, race, sexuality or religion' (Great Britain, Parliament, House of Lords, 2013a). Although this is a valuable addition to protect vulnerable victims, the chosen characteristics do not fully align to those set out in wider hate crime legislation (incorporating disability, transgender identity, race, religion and sexual orientation). Therefore, it appears that the intention to 'put victims first' is not matched by the knowledge or understanding of how to do this effectively. Consequently, it seems the championing of victims is little more than a PR exercise with the Coalition's real priorities lying elsewhere.

DOI: 10.1057/9781137409270.0010

Reflections on the Coalition's modifications

The myriad amendments, in addition to existing changes to ASB legislation, are tough on victims, but difficulties also abound for practitioners
working in the ASB field who have to act as a conduit between victim
and offender, managing perceptions and expectations for action from
both sides. Practitioners were already finding it difficult to achieve this
under the old legislation (Heap, 2010). This feeds into a broader mine-
field of public confidence in practitioners and wider statutory agencies
to deliver an effective service to reduce ASB, which will become increasingly difficult to achieve following the accepted amendments to IPNAs.
Public perceptions of practitioners' ability to stop ASB have shown there
is already a feeling that authorities' 'hands are tied', with the feeling that
nothing could be done to stop the victimization (ibid.).

The reforms to 'put victims first' have been in a state of disarray as
they progressed through the legislative process, demonstrating a failure
to achieve their original aim. The original IPNA measures were not
favourable to perpetrators or the wider public due to the potential for
groups to be marginalized and their freedom of speech constrained.
Post-amendment the new injunction powers vary little from their
predecessors, which have been categorically denounced over a number
of years for failing to effectively address the problems with ASB. This
leaves little benefit for victims; if anything the reforms have made the
ASB 'system' more difficult to navigate. In one of the final sessions in the
Commons, the Labour MP for Warrington North, Helen Jones captures
these sentiments (HL Debate 2013/14):

> the Bill still weakens the powers against antisocial behaviour, which is of
> growing concern to people. It is a badly worded Bill thrown together on the
> usual principle of, 'We must do something. This is something. Therefore,
> we must do it', which the Government seem to operate under. Large parts of
> the Bill will not offer people the protection they need.

A final detail to ruminate on is the timing of these policy changes,
particularly the presence of such long gaps between the first mention
of scrapping the ASBO in July 2010, the consultation being released in
February 2011 and the White Paper in May 2012. The English riots of
August 2011 may have been a factor, but not to an extent to warrant such
a delay. Based on the knowledge that ASB policy proved popular with
voters for New Labour (there were new policies before both the 2001 and
2005 elections), it is possible that the Coalition held back the reforms to

DOI: 10.1057/9781137409270.0010

use when they needed a popularity boost, given that the current reforms were released to coincide with news of a double-dip recession in April 2012 (BBC News, 2012) and the poor showing for the Coalition parties in the local council elections of early May 2012 (Boffey and Helm, 2012). Whilst somewhat speculative, the timing was certainly convenient and potentially indicative of the argument put forward in this book that victims are increasingly being seen as vote winners.

To summarize, this policy reformulation can be characterized as a broadening of the criminological gaze to focus on targeted, harmful or annoying behaviours which, although not strictly criminal, resonate strongly with calls for enhanced punitively minded responses from police and politicians. Similar issues are presented in the following section, with a focus on current development in responding to hate crime victimization.

Focus on: hate crime

Whilst there is no such thing as a legally defined 'hate crime', the term exists to depict acts or behaviours which are motivated in some way by the perpetrator's hostility towards the victim's actual or perceived affiliation to one (or more) of five demarcated identity categories: race, religion, sexual orientation, disability and gender identity. Hate incidents and crimes are subjectively perceived as such by the victim or any other person. The Association of Chief Police Officers (ACPO, 2010) depicts a hate incident as being 'any incident, which may or may not constitute a criminal offence, which is perceived by the victim or any other person, as being motivated by prejudice or hate' and a hate crime as being the same as this, but constituting a criminal offence. In terms of being victim-focused, this broad operational definition allows for a greater volume of incidents and crimes to be captured and then filtered out, as opposed to being missed off the radar in the early stages of the CJS.

Despite discursively 'existing' for approximately two decades, the term 'hate crime' has rapidly become a useful short-hand way of referring to acts of targeted victimization and their related offences (Perry, 2001; Garland and Chakraborti, 2009). Perry (2001: 10) offers the following useful and informative definition which has become commonplace as a starting point of analysis in hate crime scholarship:

DOI: 10.1057/9781137409270.0010

> [Hate Crime] involves acts of violence and intimidation, usually directed toward already stigmatized and marginalized groups. As such, it is a mechanism of power and oppression, intended to reaffirm the precarious hierarchies that characterize a given social order. It attempts to recreate simultaneously the threatened (real or imagined) hegemony of the perpetrator's group and the 'appropriate' subordinate identity of the victim's group. It is a means of marking both the Self and the Other in such a way as to re-establish their 'proper' relative positions, as given and reproduced by broader ideologies and patterns of social and political inequality.

Much has been written about various aspects of hate crime and related legislative responses in the UK (see Garland and Chakraborti, 2009; Duggan, 2013, 2014; Hall, 2013; Schweppe, 2012).

This section focuses on two key areas of contemporary hate crime policy. First is the Coalition's proposal to strengthen punitive sanctions for less-criminalized forms of hate crime. The analysis examines the degree to which such recommendations are based, as they claim, on a desire to promote victim equality, visibility and confidence in the criminal justice system's ability to address hate crime in a fitting manner whilst being mindful of the use such a strategy provides for the government to further their own punitive penal agendas. Second is the state's insistence on victims seeking redress through the aforementioned criminal justice route, promoting this as the appropriate way in which to avail themselves of 'justice'. Given that hate crimes encompass additional harms and impacts compared to non-targeted forms of victimization (Iganksi, 2002) encouraging victim engagement in a justice system which is notorious for focusing on process and procedure rather than addressing victims' needs is questionable in light of the restorative benefits of the punitive form of 'justice' on offer.

Origins and developments

During the 1990s, when discussions around the pros and cons of understanding victimization as being different if an identity characteristic were being targeted, the most vocal opposition to the codification of such experiences within specific legislation came from James Jacobs and Kimberly Potter (1998). They asserted that the enactment of laws designed to address hate (or 'bias', as it is often referred to in America) indicated more of a political desire to keep the general population happy as opposed to having any real impact on harm reduction or crime

DOI: 10.1057/9781137409270.0010

prevention. Most crimes, they suggested, could be seen as comprising of *some* element of hate, prejudice, bias or targeting. Nonetheless, on the whole politicians' granting of such legislation meant that they would be seen as 'doing the right thing' in addressing most victims, harm, crime and bigotry in a seemingly 'new' form of legislation. Moreover, it could be done with limited expenditure.

Legislation pertaining to UK hate crime expanded during New Labour's administration with the emergence of laws addressing targeted victimization differently according to the nature and type of the incident, as well as the relevant jurisdiction (laws in England and Wales differ slightly to Northern Ireland and to Scotland). For the purposes of this section, legislation and policy pertaining only to England and Wales are addressed. Although subsumed under a shared term, not all forms of hate crime are subject to the same laws or punishments. In the UK there currently exists a two-tier system; this is best understood as comprising crimes seen to be 'aggravated' by hostility (note that the legislation refers to hostility, not hate) and crimes where sentences are 'enhanced' due to hostility. The former relate to racial and religious hostility only and the latter recognize sexual orientation, disability and gender identity. Therefore, hierarchies of hate crime victims exist, ranked differently to *all* victims of crime, and to other forms of hate crime (Garland and Chakraborti, 2009).

The first of these pieces of legislation was the Crime and Disorder Act 1998, which outlines nine 'basic' offences that, when motivated by hostility on the grounds of race or religion, become 'aggravated' offences. The nine offences are grievous bodily harm; actual bodily harm; assault and battery; destroying or damaging property; threatening, abusive or insulting conduct towards someone with intent to cause fear of violence or provocation of violence; threatening, abusive or insulting conduct intended to cause harassment, alarm or distress; threatening, abusive or insulting conduct likely to cause harassment, alarm or distress; harassment and stalking; and putting people in fear of violence. The aggravating factor can be either demonstrated by the perpetrator (for example, through words, gestures or behaviours) or can be used to indicate his or her motivation (for example, through the victims' affiliation to an identifiable group). A person charged with one of these 'aggravated' offences may incur a higher sentence as a result of this hostility as Table 3.1 indicates.

DOI: 10.1057/9781137409270.0010

TABLE 3.1   *Basic and aggravated offences and maximum penalties*

Basic offence	Maximum penalty	Aggravated offence	Maximum penalty
Malicious wounding	5 years	Aggravated malicious wounding	7 years
Actual bodily harm	5 years	Aggravated actual bodily harm	7 years
Common assault	6 months	Aggravated common assault	2 years
Criminal damage	10 years	Aggravated criminal damage	14 years
Fear or provocation of violence	6 months	Aggravated fear or provocation of violence	2 years
Harassment, alarm or distress	Fine of up to £1,000	Aggravated harassment, alarm or distress	Fine of up to £2,500
Causing intentional harassment, alarm or distress	6 months	Aggravated causing intentional harassment, alarm or distress	2 years
Offence of harassment	6 months	Aggravated offence of harassment	2 years
Putting people in fear of violence	5 years	Aggravated putting people in fear of violence	7 years

By comparison, sections 145 and 146 of the Criminal Justice Act 2003 allow for 'enhanced sentencing' whereby a judge can increase an offender's sentence for any offence deemed to have been motivated by hostility or involving a demonstration of hostility on the basis of *any* of the five aforementioned characteristics (race, religion, sexual orientation, disability or gender identity). Usually, however, this legislation is used to address hostility pertaining to sexual orientation or disability, and now gender identity as well. The enhanced sentence does not increase the maximum sentence available, but instead allows for a higher sentence within the range set for the offence to be imparted. This is a matter of judicial discretion but must be stated in the sentencing decision announced in court.

The Public Order Act 1986 relates to the stirring up of hatred on the grounds of race, later amended to include religion in 2007 and sexual orientation in 2010. The perimeters of what can be considered 'stirring up hatred' were initially defined in the Public Order Act 1986 as including using threatening, abusive or insulting words or behaviour or displaying written material which is threatening, abusive or insulting; publishing or distributing written material which is threatening, abusive or insulting; presenting or directing the public performance of a play involving the use of threatening, abusive or insulting words or behaviour; distributing, showing or playing a recording of visual images or sounds which

DOI: 10.1057/9781137409270.0010

are threatening, abusive or insulting; providing a programme service, or producing or directing a programme, where the programme involves threatening, abusive or insulting visual images or sounds, or using the offending words or behaviour therein; or possessing written material, or a recording of visual images or sounds, which is threatening, abusive or insulting, with a view to it being displayed, published, distributed, shown, played or included in a cable programme service (Public Order Act 1986, ss. 18–23). The addition of religion and sexual orientation led to a tightening of these perimeters, with the additional information being outlined: the words or conduct must be threatening (not merely abusive or insulting); there must have been an intention to stir up hatred (a likelihood that it might be stirred up is not enough); and there are express provisions protecting freedom of expression covering, for example, criticism of religious beliefs or sexual conduct.

So far the Coalition have not sought to dismantle any of these established laws; indeed with the most recent addition of gender identity to section 146 of the Criminal Justice Act 2003, they have indicated that this framework might be strengthened and expanded to include a wider remit of behaviours and selected identities. Therefore, in a similar guise to the current debates surrounding ASB policy, hate crime – also initially established under New Labour – is being reconsidered within an enhanced punitive paradigm which seeks to impose greater punishments for demarcated victims or types of victimization. Increased punishments do not necessarily prevent crime, nor do they necessarily address victims' needs. In the cases of racist, religious and homophobic crimes (and potentially those involving hostility towards disability and gender identity too), it may be the case that imprisoning people with such prejudices for longer periods of time may reinforce such hostilities, either in a retributive sense (towards the CJS and the victim or their community) or in a situational sense (through being surrounded by others who potentially share such problematic sentiments). Increased punishments do, however, provide useful *symbolic* gestures to victims and wider society about the perceived severity of particular offences (or the targeting of particular victims). While this might prove beneficial at the time of sentencing, making it to the latter stages of the CJS in order for the symbolic punishment to be applied is not necessarily guaranteed.

Annual statistics indicate that hate crimes regularly represent approximately 1 per cent of all police recorded crime. In the 2011/2012 period, the police recorded 43,748 hate crimes, which was similar to the 2012/2013

DOI: 10.1057/9781137409270.0010

period, when 42,236 hate crime offences were recorded, resulting in a combined figure of 85,984 offences across all strands for both years (Home Office, 2013). Compared to the combined victimization data from the Crime Survey of England and Wales (CSEW) for 2011/12 and 2012/13, the approximate number of hate crimes on average per year across the five monitored strands stood at 278,000, over *three times* more than the police recorded crimes for the same two-year period detailed above. Further breakdowns for 2011/12 and 2012/13 indicate that race is by far the most common type of hate crime recorded by the police (between 82% and 85%) followed by sexual orientation (10%) then religion (4%) disability (4%) and transgender (1%) (Home Office, 2013). Hate crime reporting to the police appears consistent across years, but more telling is the huge number of incidents not being reported which are instead showing up in victimization surveys. For these victims, no amount of enhanced sentencing is going to assist them if the problem lies with the entry, not exit, point of the CJS.

For those who do report hate crime, prosecution figures indicate pursuing a case offers a good chance of securing a conviction. A report published by the Crown Prosecution Service (CPS) stated that they brought forth prosecutions for 14,196 hate crimes during the period 2011/12, and successfully prosecuted 11,843 cases during this time (some of which may include prosecutions which began prior to 2011) (CPS, 2012). However, a more detailed analysis of these prosecution figures is rendered problematic by the fact that they are not indicative of the number of times the aggravated or stirring up offences were prosecuted, the outcome of such prosecutions, or whether enhanced sentencing was applied and, if so, with what effect, as there is currently no system in place across the criminal justice system for capturing such information. Furthermore, for a hate crime prosecution to be considered 'successful', it must have been flagged *at some point* as a hate crime by the CPS in its internal records system and have resulted in some form of conviction (which may or may not reflect the hate element at this end point).

There is a much to be done by way of understanding more about the nature of hate crime prosecutions, their impact on victims and offenders and the reasons why some may prove more successful (in prosecution terms) than others. Although as indicated above, little detail is available about them and even less information is known about perpetrators. As a result of this, much of the hate crime research and scholarship focuses on victims. Even here, more information is known about some victims

DOI: 10.1057/9781137409270.0010

than others. The demographics noted by the CSEW with regards to the risk of being a victim of personal hate crime in 2011/12 and 2012/13 mirrored those for risk of victimization generally. For the most part, this involves being a single, unemployed person, usually male, aged 16–24, who religiously identifies as Muslim or 'other', and is usually from a Black or minority ethnic background (Home Office, 2013: 14). Therefore, it would seem as though this demographic are vulnerable to victimization generally, whether or not there is an identity prejudice evident. However, as mentioned previously, a key indicator separating out hate crimes from non-hate crimes is the additional impact affiliated with being targeted on the basis of identity characteristics. With regards to this impact, the 2012/13 CSEW indicated that over two-thirds (68%) of hate crime victims said they were more likely to be emotionally affected by the incident 'very much' or 'quite a lot' compared to more than one-third (37%) of victims of overall crime being emotionally affected (Home Office, 2013). Importantly in terms of exposure to secondary victimization, for those who did avail of measures to seek justice through statutory means, clear discrepancies in satisfaction rates were evident. Of those who reported their experiences through official channels, just over half (53%) of hate crime victims were likely to be satisfied by the police handling of the incident compared to nearly three-quarters (72%) of victims of overall crime who indicated a similar level of police satisfaction (Home Office, 2013). The potential for targeted victims of hostility to face *secondary* harms as a result of an unsatisfactory engagement with the CJS brings with it a whole host of additional problems which, again, render the enhancement of punishments for offending ineffective for victims of hate crime. However, it would appear to account for why this group has now been prioritized for enhanced services from the CJS, as outlined in the most recent Code (Ministry of Justice, 2013).

In March 2012, the government published *Challenge It, Report It, Stop It: The Government's Plan to Tackle Hate Crime*. This document outlined three key objectives: to prevent hate crime happening in the first place; to increase victims' willingness to report and access to support; and to improve operational responses to hate crimes. To implement these aims, plans to improve the ways in which hate crimes are recorded were outlined alongside the objective to develop a better understanding of hate victimization. This three-year action plan indicated a commitment to preventing hate crime by challenging problematic attitudes, improving early interventions to prevent hate incidents from escalating,

DOI: 10.1057/9781137409270.0010

increasing public confidence in reporting and seeking access to support, and enhancing operational responses by better identifying and managing cases, and dealing more effectively with offenders (HM Government, 2012). Efforts to address the prevention aspect of hate crime largely involved continuing support to existing practice, although ten of the 16 action points detailed a new or enhanced intervention designed to prevent victimization from occurring. The responsive aims, as well as aiming to deal effectively with offenders, have formed the basis for tougher or enhanced sentencing proposals. The next section provides an exploration of whether supposedly victim-oriented measures are really smokescreens for an increasingly system-oriented punitive agenda.

Addressing hate crime through harsher punishments

Following the Coalition's 2012 *Challenge Hate Crime* publication, the Ministry of Justice tasked the Law Commission with holding public consultations on the issue of updating or amending existing hate crime legislation applicable to England and Wales. In sum, they were to find out public opinion on extending the aggravated offences in the Crime and Disorder Act 1998 to include where hostility is demonstrated towards people on the grounds of disability, sexual orientation or gender identity; and, investigating the case for extending the stirring up of hatred offences under the Public Order Act 1986 to include disability or gender identity.

The enquiry was not required to address the rationale for the existing offences, or to consider whether the current legislation should be extended beyond the five protected characteristics. However, the Law Commission was permitted to examine the current sentencing regime applicable to cases where hostility is established, as this already applies to all five groups and involves similar elements to the aggravated offences. A key area of enquiry underpinning the investigation was whether existing criminal offences provide adequate protection against the types of wrongdoing occurring against members of the protected groups. The notion of 'protection' was evident throughout the *Challenge Hate Crime* report, whereby protection was outlined in terms of the legislation available. This proves interesting from a victimological perspective as the existence of legal sanctions alone may offer some form of *recourse* or *redress* for victimization, but potentially little *protection* from becoming a victim in the first place.

DOI: 10.1057/9781137409270.0010

Nonetheless, initial consultations with advocates representing groups included in section 146 of the Criminal Justice Act 2003 but excluded from the Crime and Disorder Act 1998 resulted in early recommendations that an adequate *response* to offences involving hostility on the grounds of disability, sexual orientation and transgender identity could be ensured if the provisions were properly applied and resulted in improved methods of recording incidents. This led the Law Commission to propose two recommendations, one regarding the establishment of a new Sentencing Council guideline dealing exclusively with hostility based on any of the five characteristics under sections 145 and 146 of the Criminal Justice Act 2003, and the other focused on recording the application of sections 145 or 146 of the Criminal Justice Act 2003 on the offender's criminal record and on the Police National Computer (Law Commission Report, 2013: 8). These recommendations focus largely on the procedural factors affecting victims of hate crime navigating through the CJS. However, they can be seen as victim-focused in the sense that having a motivating factor recognized on an offender's criminal record would address gaps in prosecution data (as detailed above), thus providing more information to victims about what forms of hate victimization are more successfully prosecuted. In addition, noting the application of sections 145 or 146 on an offender's record may alert others to the risk of future hostility if such information were to be disclosed (for example, on applications for employment).

The Law Commission's report also indicated that the enhanced sentencing regime under section 146 may prove to be an insufficient solution in cases where the conduct in issue is not criminal (for example, in the cases of hate 'incidents'). This may account for the late insertion of hate crime in ASB policy (detailed in the above section) to capture this cohort. The consultation did not, however, address extending the aforementioned legislation to cover *new* groups (for example, hostility based on biological gender, age, engagement in sex work, homelessness or class).[2] This fails to consider scholarship highlighting the exclusionary and discriminatory nature of categorizations among and outside of those selected for an enhanced criminal justice focus (Schweppe, 2012). It could be argued that if the government's efforts to combat identity-based victimization or targeted harassment and violence were truly victim oriented, they would be looking at addressing such victimization from the basis of additional forms of identity (such as those outlined above), or the offender's expression of hostility towards *any* given factor (for example, the victim's job). Instead, segregating crime types according to the actual or perceived group affiliation of the target victim creates hierarchies whereby some forms of hostility are treated as 'worse' than others. This brings with it a plethora of problems, not least when the victim embodies more than one of the identity characteristics noted in such legislation but can only avail of one 'strand' during the CJS process. Furthermore, strengthening punishments for the most serious types of offences which segregate violent hate crime offenders from violent offenders generally not only creates false distinctions between such violent offenders (who may be one and the same person at different points in time), but may also fail to address the more pressing issue of how *violence* is conceptualized and (potentially) rationalized by perpetrators. Addressing the hostility is – of course – important, but so too is the manner in which it is manifested; there is a danger that this may be overlooked if the focus concentrates too heavily on the *motivation* for the act as opposed to the act itself. If such issues are not duly considered, then the ultimate impact will be felt by any future victim who may be subjected to sustained or heightened levels of violence as a result of a perpetrator's prejudice or hostility. Increasing the length of sentences for demonstrations of identity hostility during more serious levels of harm may be politically symbolic but the degree to which they assist with the prevention of victimization remains to be seen.

In a somewhat contradictory fashion to the established legal framework, the most recent report into hate crime in the UK produced by the Home Office (2013: 11) states that: 'Crimes based on hostility to age, gender, or appearance, for example, can also be hate crimes, although they are not part of the five centrally monitored strands.' Confusion over what constitutes a hate crime is something police forces have been seeking to address through awareness-raising campaigns (Duggan, 2014). Public information leaflets and posters have been designed to increase knowledge around hate crime and to boost confidence in reporting such incidents. These efforts may, in part, be rendered more difficult given the Home Office's statement above which appears to foreground the presence of *any* form of hate or hostility, rather than those affiliated to a demarcated group. The conceptualization of identity is still indicated (gender, age, appearance) but may confuse the public further with regards to whether or not they are a victim of hate crime, or can avail themselves of the available legislation.

DOI: 10.1057/9781137409270.0010

However, the Home Office were not the first to broaden such definitions; on at least one occasion a sentencing judge used his discretion to indicate that an offence was motivated by hatred of a person's difference, identity or characteristics. Following the murder of Sophie Lancaster in 2007, the judge drew on the alternative appearance embodied by Sophie and her boyfriend Robert Maltby (who survived the attack) when describing the act as being a 'hate crime' (in this case, against the Goth subculture) during his summing up of the trial (Garland, 2010). A victim-focused approach to addressing hate or hostility from the perspective of a responsive criminal justice system would suggest that demarcated identity categories are dismantled on the basis of being exclusive and limiting. Alluding to situations similar to the Sophie Lancaster trial, Schweppe (2012: 182–183) describes this as a 'depoliticizing' of the hate crime trial process:

> [J]uries (or triers of fact) [should] determine whether, on the basis of the evidence before them, a hate crime was committed, rather than curtailing the operation of the legislation to a limited number of (albeit fully deserving) victim groups.

Several factors are pertinent to note here. First, the identified groups who can legitimately claim to have been victims of hate crime have generally been selected on the basis of historical socio-legal persecutions. For example, 'race' is a demarcated category, and – as noted above – regularly comprises the largest number of reported victims of the five discernable groups in official and unofficial statistics. When broken down further, it appears that within this overarching category of 'race', the highest proportion of targeted victimization is experienced by members of Black and minority ethnic (as opposed to White) communities (Home Office, 2013). However, the legislation pertaining to racial hatred does not stipulate that the victim has to be from a minority racial group, nor does it state that the hate crime perpetrator(s) should be from a dominant majority group (or, indeed, a different racial group).[3] Given the ethnicity dynamic, hate crime can occur within races but across ethnic divides. Therefore, instances of racial hate crime victimization whereby ethnic differences fuel tensions *within*, as opposed to *between*, minority or majority racial cohorts, are less visible as a result of a popular 'dominant versus minority' conceptualization of who is perpetrating and experiencing hate crime.

DOI: 10.1057/9781137409270.0010

Similarly, the proportion of White (Caucasian) victims availing of relevant racial legislative protections remains low; this could represent a lower likelihood of incurring racial victimization, a lower level of awareness of the applicability of the legislation as a form of criminal justice redress, or a lower level of willingness to seek justice for harms incurred in this manner. The 'victim-focused' nature of hate crime legislation and policy is illustrated via the focus on the victim's identity characteristics, but in punishing the offender's hostility more harshly on this basis then these victims are also being used to enhance retributive penal sanctions.

When applied to victimization on the basis of religious or sexual orientation hostility, the focus on minority groups is similarly evident. The targeting of Muslims increased significantly following the murder of soldier Lee Rigby in Woolwich in May 2013 (*The Guardian*, 2013). This selective targeting is rendered more visible as Muslims make up just 5 per cent of the population (Census, 2011). Christians, at 59 per cent of the population, rarely feature as recorded victims of religious hate crime so it is likely that the majority of religious hate crime is directed towards Muslims or those perceived to be Muslims (most likely through inferences based on their appearance). Although anti-Semitic attacks can also be classed as religious hostility, Judaism is most usually seen to comprise an ethnicity thus is more likely to be categorized in hate crime statistics as being racially motivated. Therefore, if a disproportionate amount of religiously motivated hate crime were being targeted towards one particular religious group, a 'victim-focused' response might involve the greater deployment of resources and efforts addressing *that* particular form of hostility (not unlike the 'target hardening' crime prevention approaches discussed earlier), ultimately proving more beneficial to both the CJS and members of this community who perceive themselves to be at risk of targeted victimization. Of the 16 prevention recommendations in the *Challenge Hate Crime* report, only two are partially aimed at achieving this.

A similar set of circumstances can be seen with regards to sexual orientation. Between 5 and 10 per cent of the population identify as lesbian, gay or bisexual, meaning that the percentage of sexual orientation victimization recorded by a variety of surveys (Dick, 2008; Home Office 2013) is disproportionately focused on sexual minorities. However, it has been noted in most studies that gay men are more likely to be targeted for victimization than lesbian women, with bisexuals

DOI: 10.1057/9781137409270.0010

of either gender reporting fewer experiences in total. With the more notable cases of homophobic hostility in the UK depicting male victims (such as Jody Dubrowski and Ian Baynham, mentioned earlier) and more men than women being represented in hate crime statistics, it is important that a 'victim-focused' approach to this particular type of targeted victimization accounts for gender. This is important both to effectively address crimes against gay men and to not render lesbian women even more invisible in criminal justice discourses and initiatives. Despite inferences to the contrary being outlined by the Home Office report above, gender as a distinct category is currently not *officially* recognized as a basis from which to experience hate crime. While gender identity has recently been formally included in section 146 legislation (through the Legal Aid, Punishment and Sentencing of Offenders Act, 2012), this only applies to people who have switched from their gender identity at birth. Challenging homophobia and transphobia in sport is the only explicit reference to this particular type of hate crime in the *Challenge Hate Crime* report; where not indicative of a target population, one assumes that homophobia and transphobia will be included in the initiatives designed to address prejudice as a whole.

Reflections on the Coalition's modifications

Historic rationales for hate crime policy and legislation were founded on the wishes of minority groups who lobbied government to enact legislation that would offer legal protections from discrimination (see, for example, the Equality Act 2010) or offer legal redress for harms incurred as a result of perpetrator prejudice (such as the Acts detailed earlier in this section). However, despite their (sometimes vast) differences, the homogenizing of minority groups under 'umbrella' terms such as 'hate crime' can be problematic. Some minority groups are more vocal than others, so caution is needed when the needs and wants of a discernable group are transposed onto all groups. This may also be a consideration for policy makers seeking to enhance legislation along more punitive lines. Research by Mason-Bish (2010) illustrates this, indicating how representatives from disability organizations felt compelled to follow in the footsteps of race, religion and sexual orientation groups and request that disability be included in hate crime legislation in order to be seen as politically relevant and included in prejudice-related decisions.

DOI: 10.1057/9781137409270.0010

Disablist hate crime can take very different forms and be motivated by very different factors compared to the other strands (Sherry, 2010). This has led to concerns being raised over whether expanding current legislation will negatively impact on victims of disablist hate crime, either through failing to address the economic exploitation evident in many cases, or dissuading victims who have an interpersonal relationship with the perpetrator (for example, being their primary carer) who fear having to enter residential care if their abuser is imprisoned for a lengthy period of time.

Relying on identity categorizations also poses problems of a different kind. Hall (2013) illustrates that restricting hate crime to just focus on victimization experienced by members of minority groups might address problems of expansion (whereby *everyone* falls under *some* form of protection, thus renders the legislation meaninglessness). However, on the other side of the coin, selective exclusion may be interpreted by some as a signifier of worthlessness. Returning to the majority/minority issues detailed above, Chakraborti (2010) adds that additional problems may occur if racial victimization experienced by a member of a dominant ethnic community were not recognized by the CJS in any circumstances. From an anecdotal perspective (based on one of the authors' engagement with criminology undergraduate students), it appears that some people consider themselves precluded from availing themselves of hate crime legislation on the basis of not embodying a minority identity, even though they do not need to identify as such as a hate crime is dependent on the victim (or any other person) perceiving it through the perpetrator demonstrating some form of hostility to their identity. If experiences of hate crime by members of dominant identity groups (for example, White people, Christians or heterosexuals) were overlooked, then this could feed into harmful propaganda which suggests that minority groups are given 'special treatment' in the CJS.

This perspective was demonstrated in a report produced by David Green, founder of the independent think-tank, Civitas: The Institute for the Study of Civil Society. In the report, Green (2006) took issue with the separating out of different types of victim experience at all, particularly on the basis of identity. He suggested that the demands made of minority groups upon law and policy is tantamount to special treatment, thus was unfair on the rest of society. In his analysis, he interestingly bands together *all* minority identities in one single cohort, including women, in order to indicate that 'minorities' actually

DOI: 10.1057/9781137409270.0010

comprise of a holistic majority when considered in this manner. In his critique of the increasingly politicized nature of 'victimhood', Green (2006: 1) states:

> [T]oday to be classified as a victim is to be given a special political status, which has no necessary connection with real hardship or actual oppression. Victimhood as a political status is best understood as the outcome of a political strategy by some groups aimed at gaining preferential treatment. In free societies groups often organise to gain advantages for themselves, but the increase in the number and power of groups seeking politically-mandated victim-hood raises some deeper questions.

Green's focus on those subject to policy rather than those creating it shifts the focus onto the contemporary power and influence of victims and their advocates. His claims to the emergence of 'victimocracy', which he defines as 'the emergence of rule by victim groups' (Green, 2006: 4) coupled with his suggestion that politicized victim status does not necessarily correlate to oppression is problematic for two main reasons. First, it negates victims' lived experiences of (and statistics relating to) racism, religious hostility, homophobia, transphobia and disablist hate crime as being a real and valid issue. Being persecuted on the basis of an inherent, immutable or intrinsic characteristic may impact some people more than the actual victimizing behaviour. Second, it negates the historical factors informing the socio-legal and political persecution of people on these bases as a result of seeing minorities as second-class citizens or criminally deviant. Social constructions of people as acceptable targets for victimization or prejudice were reinforced by laws which either directly discriminated against them or protected those who demonstrated bias. Therefore, a similar form of symbolism may be found in reversing these laws to target the persecutor, rather than the persecuted. Although this may be what Green means by 'preferential treatment', his failure to detail what he means by this specifically renders it unclear. It is the case that some local policing policies have outlined enhanced measures for interacting with hate crime victims; for example, South Yorkshire Police aim to make initial contact victims who have reported hate crime within one hour (Duggan and Heap, 2013). Whether or not this amounts to 'preferential treatment', or a concerted effort to engage otherwise reluctant victims, is debatable. Nonetheless, if examples such as this are evidence of Green's suggestion of a move towards a 'victimocracy', then it is little

DOI: 10.1057/9781137409270.0010

wonder that the Coalition desires to harness this surge of momentum around socio-legal advances in victim visibility.

Significant gaps exist in current information on hate crime prosecutions and offenders, as well as on the impact of prosecutions on victims and their communities. Recognizing that at the very least a hate crime victim may want to see *some* form of prosecution, the CPS has suggested changes which may increase the chances of this happening. For example, cases which are heard in the magistrates' courts are precluded from availing of the option to return an alternative verdict of guilty of a lesser or alternative offence. Therefore, if a racially aggravated offence is charged, and the racial aggravation is subsequently not proven, the defendant will be acquitted even if there is proof of the basic offence. The proposed changes would result in both the basic *and* the racially or religiously aggravated offences being charged, in effect doubling the chances of a prosecution. This may prove advantageous for hate crime victims seeking a 'successful' outcome, but may carry negative consequences due to the omission of the aggravating element if they desire this to be recognized. On the other hand, such a move would again render hate crimes different in that an offender would be charged with two offences, possibly leading opponents to invoke claims of 'preferential treatment' and a departure from the due process model. Herein lies a discord between being focused on the best outcome for the victim and the fairest outcome for the offender and CJS.

To summarize, it would appear that New Labour's approach to identifying targeted and repeat forms of victimization in the form of ASB and hate crime discourses, laws and policies has been appropriated by the Coalition to underpin their much-hyped 'victim-focused' agenda. Within these two policy domains, victims' needs and wants have been co-opted to epitomize a desire for greater levels of criminal justice engagement (particularly for non-criminal incidents) either to involve victims at the early stages of troublesome behaviour (ASB) or to use their experiences to underpin tougher sentencing (hate crime). This in turn has instigated practices resulting in harsher sentences for offenders based on *motivators* for crime (such as targeting vulnerability or on the basis of identity) as opposed to focusing more attention on the criminal act itself. While these efforts may be rooted in a desire to promote a robust, fit-for-purpose criminal justice system within which those affected by crime can avail themselves of 'justice', whether or not this leads to a 'satisfactory outcome' for the victim remains questionable

DOI: 10.1057/9781137409270.0010

as their experience of being subject to ASB or hate-based victimization may well continue. Rather than lessening the chances of being affected by crime, the government instead appears intent on improving the victim experience of the criminal justice system. In other words, these policies variously aim to administrate victimization through managing victims' experiences of, and engagement with, the system rather than reduce their likelihood of having to encounter it in the first place. In this vein, when governments speak of 'victims' policies' and 'putting victims first', they are acknowledging that victims are a guaranteed cohort to whom attention should be paid. *Being* a victim of crime, therefore, is not in question. Instead, efforts to address victims through policy are beginning to indicate a greater concern with what happens to them during the process *afterwards*, when the responsibility has shifted to the CJS.

Summary of key points

- ▸ Developments in ASB policy have expanded the nature and scope of available measures and responses.
- ▸ Being targeted for victimization, or being deemed a vulnerable victim, is becoming more significant in shaping the type of statutory response enacted.
- ▸ Hate crime policy consultations have suggested enhancing the severity of legal sanctions for lesser-criminal forms of targeted victimization to equalize these with existing 'aggravated' offences.
- ▸ The role and status of ASB and hate crime victims have become more prominent within criminal justice frameworks but necessitate engagement with the CJS in order to access the measures available.

Notes

1 This does, of course, assume a rational offender, which is not without extensive limitations (see Downes and Rock, 2011).
2 Schweppe (2012: 177) outlines a list of recognized forms of hate crime in the United States which also include citizenship, economic status, family responsibility, matriculation, membership of Labour organization, marital

DOI: 10.1057/9781137409270.0010

status, national origin, personal appearance, political orientation or affiliation, sex and social status.

3   This was decided in the case of *White* [2001] EWCA Crim 216, [2001] 1 WLR 1352 but not in the case of *DPP v Pal* [2000] Criminal Law Review 756. In the latter case, words used by the defendant inferred that the victim (both of Asian origin) was betraying his own racial group through his associations with others (who were White).

DOI: 10.1057/9781137409270.0010

4
Reconceptualizing Victims

Abstract: *Chapter 4 suggests that a reconceptualization of victims and victimization has emerged. Processes of politicization in contemporary victim policy have constructed new hierarchies of victimization whereby certain victims face enhanced levels of criminal justice bureaucratization, whilst others have been overlooked entirely. These victim hierarchies have been reconstructed along three lines: demarcation, prioritization and responsibilization. Although extolled as being part of a wider 'victim-focused' agenda, this instead indicates a move towards administrating victimization whereby current victim policy seeks to manage the victim experience in the CJS in line with the dominant political ideology underpinning current developments in criminal justice. The chapter concludes by considering how victims currently feature in wider political rhetoric and calls for a renewed victimological focus on administrated victimization.*

Keywords: administration; deservedness; general election; hierarchized victimization; victims' rights; vulnerability

Duggan, Marian and Vicky Heap. *Administrating Victimization: The Politics of Anti-Social Behaviour and Hate Crime Policy.* Basingstoke: Palgrave Macmillan, 2014. DOI: 10.1057/9781137409270.0011.

The preceding chapters have sought to present an argument that contemporary developments in victims' policy place a particular emphasis on engaging victims as stakeholders in the criminal justice system (CJS) through a variety of means, not least through providing numerous conduits through which 'victims' voices' are channelled. Reconceptualizations of victims as consumer stakeholders advanced under New Labour appear to be intensified with the Coalition government; despite evidence that recorded crime is falling, victims have become an increasingly important form of currency for political parties, particularly those with a staunch law and order agenda. Rather than trying to control crime, policies appear to be attempting to control the victim experience. *Being a victim of crime*, therefore, is taken as read; efforts to address victims through policy indicate a greater concern with what happens to them *afterwards*, so long as this can be processed through the CJS. Guidelines ensure that victims seek redress or resolution via the criminal justice system, accessing services which are increasingly likely to be tendered out to the private sector. The impact of the current economic situation is important to consider too. Advancing neoliberal, market-driven agendas through the privatization of public services proves a far more palatable approach if promoted as a means of saving taxpayers' money. This shows how victims are being considered and processed in a manner similar to that which has been witnessed with offenders under the current Transforming Rehabilitation model.

Furthermore, the increased emphasis on ensuring victim *satisfaction* during their navigation of the criminal justice process demonstrates that bureaucratizing the victim experience, and delegating responsibility for different aspects of this, is proving more manageable (and potentially achievable). Whilst promising to reduce or eliminate victimization in the first place may be difficult, relying upon its continuation does victims a disservice. These concepts reflect how the continuing impact of the Coalition's individualized, law and order ideologies alluded to earlier in the analysis have come to permeate the victim domain on individual and organizational levels. The amplification in administrating victimization through policy guidelines applies more readily to some victims than others. Despite producing Victims' Codes and Charters which purport to speak to *all* victims, the Coalition has redefined hierarchies of need which align with new considerations of vulnerability. The politically desirable contemporary 'ideal victim' is now one who can be *demarcated* along the lines of group affiliation or victimization

DOI: 10.1057/9781137409270.0011

experience and benefit from *prioritized* responses targeted at that cohort. However, these victims are also *responsibilized* to avail themselves of the resources offered for the pursuit of 'justice' or conflict resolution. The reconceptualization of victimization along socially constructed categories, such as ASB and hate crime, provides a platform from which to promote strengthened criminal justice responses, most usually aimed at increasing both the victim and the perpetrator's interaction with the CJS. Invoking Christie's (1977) thesis on the state 'stealing' conflicts in order to reassert its power and legitimacy, this reconceptualization could be viewed as indicating a much more intensified and monopolizing form of interaction; rather than having lost the right to participate in their conflict, victims of ASB and hate crime are in danger of losing the right *not* to participate.

This final chapter draws on the evidence presented throughout the book to explicitly demonstrate how neoliberal ideologies have impacted on the individualization and responsibilization of victims and their advocates in the criminal justice system. The emergence of hierarchies, and within these victim 'silos' has reignited Christie's (1986) analysis of how deservedness functions in the construction of the legitimate (or prioritized) victim identity. The analysis demonstrates how current socio-political approaches to addressing victims' needs and wants identify these as being primarily administrative in nature (for example, more transparent criminal justice processes or the ability to have more input in a trial). This belies research findings which repeatedly demonstrate that victims have additional needs not currently addressed by the CJS, or in some cases want resolutions *outside* of the CJS entirely.

The chapter also explores how victims feature in wider political rhetoric, indicating a resurgence in discussions around furnishing victims with codified 'rights'. The debate about rights emulates the increasing management of victims' experiences once in the CJS, thus prioritizing the focus on responsive action. These rights discourses emulate hierarchical policy approaches by making reference to labelled cohorts, but are focused on 'vulnerable and intimidated', not 'repeat and targeted' victims. Interestingly, the characteristics attributed to 'vulnerable and intimidated' witnesses as set out in policy guidelines are, with the exception of disability, quite distinct from those deemed to be 'repeat and targeted' victims. The following section explores this and potential future trends in victim policy, returning to the issue of whether a political approach to demarcated victimization facilitates a comfortable gap between rhetoric

DOI: 10.1057/9781137409270.0011

and reality when it comes to governments being truly willing and able to 'put victims first'.

Hierarchizing victimization

This section explores the reconceptualization of victim hierarchies, illustrating how processes which demarcate and prioritize victims according to victimization type are informed by new understandings of deservedness. This impacts on the way in which victims are interacted with during their navigation of the CJS, how they may be used to promote political agendas calling for enhanced or expanded criminalization, and who may be left out as a result of ideologies of deservedness reappearing in contemporary political reconstructions of victim identity.

Victim *demarcation* and *prioritization* are characterized by new frameworks of susceptibility to victimization which move the concept of 'vulnerability' beyond its traditional understanding. As well as previously recognizable 'risk' factors (such as age, gender or ability), additional aspects evident within ASB and hate crime discourses include being targeted on the basis of a perceived identity status (such as being an ethnic or sexual minority). Of equal note is the increased focus on repeat victimization; once largely affiliated to property crimes (such as burglary) and domestic abuse, this has expanded to include cases of interpersonal victimization, which have moved beyond traditional understandings to account for new 'types' of repeat victimization. ASB and hate crime victims, characterized by being vulnerable *and* subject to repeat incidents, now occupy a heightened status in policy formulation. Walklate (2007: 79–80) warns how targeting repeat victimization, as distinct from other forms of victimization 'is not only theoretically misplaced but also, in policy and resource effectiveness terms, only ever going to be at best partially successful'. Nonetheless, the *process* of categorizing those worthy of elevated status has changed to reflect the political saliency of certain victimization types, based on newly formed perimeters of perceived level of vulnerability surrounding repeat and vulnerable victims. Whilst the Victims' Code (2013) is meant to address *all* victims, the emphasis on victim identities and crime types that warrant an enhanced support service indicate the emergence of prioritized victims. With the changes to victims' services in light of the privatization agenda, it may prove

DOI: 10.1057/9781137409270.0011

beneficial for victims to identify within one of these demarcated lines to avail of a satisfactory response.

One form of demarcation illustrated in this book is the separating out of responses to ASB and hate crime in policy. This has occurred despite the similarities between these forms of victimization: both, for example, encompass what is often termed 'low level' victimization or harassment such as verbal abuse, intimidation, criminal damage, breach of the peace or minor assault. These behaviours are usually carried out by groups of (often young) people who are known to some degree to the victims, who then rarely report incidents to the police as a result of feeling that the CJS is incapable of assisting (Heap, 2010; Duggan and Heap, 2013). Whilst a separatist approach may prove politically advantageous, for the most vulnerable in society this tactic may (or in the case of Fiona Pilkington, indeed did) prove detrimental. The potential for duplicated information, inconsistencies in process, blurred boundaries as to what categorization might be more suitable and general misinformation regarding the action to be taken are some of the potential pitfalls of having multiple responses available for similar forms of victimization.

If such a separatist approach is to persist, then increasing public awareness of policing practices and procedures can enhance and ensure suitable responses. Within the hate crime domain, many statutory and third-sector organizations exist which are dedicated to inform-ing minority communities about criminal justice processes available to those affected by targeted victimization. By contrast, this is not as pronounced for victims of ASB, who therefore may not even bother reporting incidents in the first place if they feel that the police are unwilling or unable to help them. This may in turn mean that victims become more disillusioned with a CJS which they see as prioritizing a 'hierarchy of victimization' which is not in their favour. This is par-ticularly pertinent given that whilst the victimization may be similar in nature, the fact that the presence of identity-based hostility means one will be categorized as a 'hate crime' and the other 'anti-social behav-iour', which immediately dichotomizes the perceptions of seriousness and legality affiliated to the act.

Shifting silos

Other hierarchies may exist which are equally as problematic. The notion of 'silos' is commonplace in hate crime discourse, most usually forming

DOI: 10.1057/9781137409270.0011

part the critique against categorizing or compartmentalizing victimization along identity lines in a manner which means groups with shared objectives operate independently of one another (usually separated by identity politics) rather than interactively to address the broader issue of hate motivated victimization. A consequence of this compartmentalization of victim experiences, identities and types of harm is the ability of organizations to access limited government resources with which to address *their* particular victims' needs and wants. Identity politics is one explanation for the underdeveloped nature of cross-over or shared working practice between hate crime victims' groups. Another is the potential that instilling competitiveness between these organizations means that they are rendered more manageable through standardizing and professionalizing their working practices to enable them to compete more effectively with private sector organizations, who may also be tendering for victim service contracts.

Contrasted against these processes of demarcating along *singular* identity lines is the concept of blending identities, or addressing 'intersectionality' – different sites of identity meeting, or intersecting, to form parts of a whole. Within individuals, intersectionality most usually refers to the different identities one person will embody (for example, their race, gender, class, age). On a practitioner level, it requires addressing the different aspects of a person's identity which may have resonance in the victimization they have experienced, or render them more vulnerable to being targeted as a result of these multiple factors. Ironically, people who embody multiple minority identity factors may be more vulnerable as a result of increased susceptibility to targeted victimization, however they constitute the very victims who 'fall through the gaps' if not correctly categorized or if their experiences recognized. For example, a person who is targeted on the basis of both their sexual orientation *and* racial identity may be an example of a hidden population facing dual discrimination or multiple victimization, yet would be officially categorized on the basis of one or the other identity factors. Scholarly work on intersectionality and targeted victimization indicates how such considerations could be more effectively addressed at policy-maker level as a result of harmonizing, rather than separating out, identity-based initiatives (Duggan, 2014).

The existence of silos creates the potential for victims to fall through gaps in other ways. The system requires victims to be able to communicate their issues, needs and wants successfully in order to obtain the support

DOI: 10.1057/9781137409270.0011

or redress they seek. This in itself creates a hierarchy of victims dependent on their ability to do this. It also potentially delineates victims based on their previous experience of the system, with informed victims more able to act as consumers by strategically choosing how they interact with the CJS in order to maximize their chances of satisfaction. Linked to this is the fact that while specific advocates for hate crime victims are very apparent, the inverse is true for ASB. Despite a broad diversity of ASB victim types (as a consequence of the subjective interpretation of behaviour), they are often treated as a homogenous group. This may be a consequence of support not being considered necessary for victims of low-level, perception-based, sub-criminal behaviour in contrast to those who have been criminally victimized. Tensions exist when attempting to identify where the spectrum of victimization begins and enforcing that lowest level benchmark consistently, which has been a perennial issue since 'ASB' first emerged in 1998.

ASB silos occurred through the differential treatment of private and social housing tenants, which were previously demarcated in legislative terms by the different types of sanctions available to their perpetrators. However the type of *support* provided to such victims has been broadly similar. The is exemplified by the lack of any national victims' movements for ASB victims with local provision often established from the bottom-up, thus creating piecemeal provision for victims dependent on their residential location. Where support exists, it tends to reflect the neoliberal and responsibilization elements promoted by the Coalition. For example, the Birmingham Residents Antisocial Behaviour Victim Empowerment project was established in 2012 using Big Lottery Fund money, with the anticipation it will be delivered by volunteers from 2015 onwards aligning with the Coalition's Big Society agenda.

Dictating deservedness

The discussion above demonstrates a shift in the hierarchies of victimization which moves them on from previous conceptions of good and bad victims (Madlingozi, 2007) to categorizing people according to whose needs are seen to be most significant at the time. Furthermore, it would appear that the level of prioritization afforded to particular groups of victims relates to several additional factors, such as the level of media focus enhancing the high-profile nature of individual cases or exposing the fundamental failings of the CJS in responding to these. Using

DOI: 10.1057/9781137409270.0011

the example of hate crime within a politicized context, Walklate (2007) draws attention to how hierarchies of victim status can change over time in respect of these additional factors. This is illustrated by the rapid development of hate crime legislation following the murder of black teenager Stephen Lawrence in 1993, and the enhanced prioritization of disability as vulnerability (in the ASB agenda and elsewhere) that swiftly followed the Pilkington case. These, coupled with measures such as naming laws after deceased victims (such as Sarah's Law or Clare's Law) appear indicative of what it takes to have some forms of victimization taken seriously in political circles.

Nonetheless, governments capitalizing on high-profile cases, most usually within a remit of 'learning lessons' for the future, illustrates a response reflective of Aradau's (2004) 'politics of pity' concept. She highlights how emotions towards victims are used by governments to reconstruct and manage their situation, although the *nature* of the suffering recognized is a social construction and not necessarily reflective of any inherent value. Aradau (2004: 258) states how 'the politics of pity therefore needs to configure suffering as recognisable, something the spectators can identify and sympathise with'. Walklate (2011) notes the link between the politics of pity and Christie's (1986) ideal victim, and poses questions as to who, how and why individuals or groups become worthy of pity. The analysis and evidence provided throughout the earlier chapters in this book point to one answer for these questions: currently groups or individuals are selected based on the premise of politicized victimization (Miers, 1978). Others, however, may be so low down this hierarchy as to almost be considered unworthy of note, or are off the radar altogether. For example, Duggan (2013) indicates how apparently progressive victim measures are hindered in practice as a result of social prejudices held towards historically marginalized groups. Focusing specifically on street-sleeping homeless people (who are at a heightened level of vulnerability and risk of victimization) and Romany Gypsies and Irish Travellers, Duggan (2013) explores the victimization incurred by these groups which reinforces the undervalued position they occupy in both society and political rhetoric; rather than being seen as *more* vulnerable and in need of protection, their identities have been devalued (Gypsies and Travellers) or deemed invalid (street-sleeping homeless people). These deprioritization has also been exacerbated as a result of these two groups being unable to achieve recognition through capitalization on high-profile cases and/

DOI: 10.1057/9781137409270.0011

or grass roots activism as, for those where no cause célèbre or pressure group exists, their marginalized status quo remains.

Administrative victimization

The Coalition government's failure to consider victims in their initial programme for government was one of the biggest indicators of how relevant victims were during the early stages of this political partnership. Now, however, it may well be the case that in light of other disastrous or detrimental socio-economic and socio-political factors (as outlined in Chapter 2), deflecting attention on to what can and must be done to assist (certain) victims is enjoying a revived level of statutory interest. Victims are being subject to administrative processes emulating those which epitomize the offender's journey through the criminal justice system. Coalition policies have therefore moved beyond what Garland (1996) depicts as the normalizing of crime, to embody the *normalization of victimization*. This is reflected by policies that focus more on managing the impact of the crime event, such as the Victims' Code (2013) and the Community Trigger in ASB policy. Managing victimization appears to have become as normal as any other modern-day administrative process, such as filing a tax return or buying a house. In the same vein, there has been a shift from treating the crime problem (never mind the causes) to a type of crime policy that manages the inevitability of harm, almost analogous to palliative care in a healthcare context. If crime control policy has witnessed this shift, what beholds the justice process?

Victims are arguably becoming more involved in relation to achieving justice. This change in emphasis demonstrates the evolving nature from pre-crime to post-crime involvement, shifting the relationship between individuals and the state, whilst facilitating the opportunities for victim hierarchies to be created. This 'victim as administrator' approach embodies the neoliberalization and Big Society agendas embraced by the Coalition through requiring greater levels of active involvement and responsibility. The existence of hierarchies is compounded by the commodification of security within this neoliberal model, whereby those without the necessary financial power are marginalized. In the next section, processes of responsibilization are explored in order to assess the impact the diffusion of responsibility from the state to the individual has

DOI: 10.1057/9781137409270.0011

on levels of culpability, liability and accountability, as well as the opportunity this provides for policies designed to address the after effects of victimization.

Responsibilizing victims

There is a discord between who should be and who is responsible for addressing victims of crime. Garland (1996, 2001) suggests that there has been a broadening out with regards to who is responsible for crime control, from the government to individuals and organizations. This can be seen as illustrative of what Garland describes as a 'responsibilization strategy' (1996: 452):

> This involves the central government seeking to act upon crime not in a direct fashion through state agencies (police, courts, prisons, social work, etc.) but instead by acting indirectly, seeking to activate action on the part of non-state agencies and organizations.

Within a victimological framework, this may involve individuals, communities and organizations working to address victimization in line with dominant political ideologies. As well as focusing on crime prevention, this may also involve dealing with or managing the impact of crime once event has taken place. Another example is the emphasis on victims being encouraged to achieve a proscribed form of 'justice' through a specified CJS paradigm; reporting their experience and co-operating with any ensuing investigation.

The new focus on responsibilizing victims places an even greater emphasis on victim investment to achieve the best outcome following their victimization experience. This is required despite the potential to incur further emotional costs as a result of navigating through an increasingly bureaucratic system having already suffered a traumatic experience. There may also be financial costs at stake. For example, traditional responsibilization-led 'target hardening' crime prevention initiatives usually required victims of crime (or members of the public keen to avoid victimization) to invest in lock and bolts. With a reduction in prevention rhetoric, fewer general messages about public crime prevention are evident (for example, television adverts proclaiming messages such as 'car crime; together we'll crack it', so familiar in the 1980s and 1990s). Instead, these have been replaced with a focus on creating systems available for victims to seek redress (for example, easier reporting mechanisms, greater support promised during the investigation and

DOI: 10.1057/9781137409270.0011

trial process, redesigned compensation guidelines). These systems are designed to create a positive victim experience, a key focus for contemporary victim policy.

Mindfulness towards victim satisfaction is not new; a similar notion was raised by Garland (1996: 456) who suggested the responsibilization strategy was concerned with 'consumer relations … and being responsive to their [victims'] expressed needs'. Top line findings from the Witness and Victim Experience Survey (which ran between 2007 and 2010) suggested the presence of strong victim satisfaction levels, with 84 per cent satisfied with their overall contact with the CJS. However, further investigation of the analysis reveals differences in experience due to crime type and personal characteristics, such as disability (Franklyn, 2012). The recommendations suggest more should be done to 'manage' victims' and witnesses' expectations, which could account for the renewed approach the Coalition has adopted regarding satisfaction levels.

However, as has been demonstrated, treating victims as a homogenous group is naïve. Laxminarayan et al. (2013) suggest there needs to be a distinction *between* victims to fully understand the factors influencing satisfaction levels. This embodies issues highlighted earlier regarding how victims of ASB or hate crime can be responded to very differently despite suffering similar types of incidents depending on whether they are classed (by the victim themselves or the authorities) as one or the other types of victimization. This places a duty on victims to get their entrance into the CJS 'right' if they were to achieve a satisfactory outcome. Consequently, this might be evidence of political moves towards creating a system whereby it is the *victims'* responsibility to 'manage' the CJS, with the necessity to become fluent at navigating a system of bureaucratic processes in order to attain their desired outcome.

The increase in process and procedure, such as the ASB Community Trigger, clearly intend to address victim satisfaction around outcomes but numerous questions remain. Victims of crime and ASB are being considered in a manner reminiscent of a 'consumer relations' approach. This would fit with the wider neoliberal remit of the Coalition, but is founded on little or no supporting evidence to suggest that this course of action is effective. Instead, it has the feel of a knee-jerk reaction to the high-profile fatalities mentioned in the Introduction. This approach allows the Coalition to be seen to be *doing something*, providing them vote-winning rhetoric which can be easily reproduced in media soundbites. However in practice, this system appears poorly conceived with

DOI: 10.1057/9781137409270.0011

truly vulnerable victims still disadvantaged in their pursuit of satisfaction due to the complexity of the process. Similar criticisms can be levied at the revised Victims' Code, updated for a third time in 2013. This document is 78 pages long, with the 'easy read' still amassing a lengthy 48 pages. The Code is supposed to 'make sure victims' voices are heard', but at a time of distress, reading through such a lengthy instruction manual to ensure you are heard is unlikely to be prioritized. This brings into question the fundamental value of the Code. A 2013 investigation of complaints into the old Code conducted by Parliamentary Ombudsman Dame Julie Mellor suggested a lack of public awareness and understanding made it of little value to victims (Mellor, 2013). With the extensive new Code, which was not launched amid a whirlwind of publicity, there is no indication this issue will be resolved thus reinforcing the problems inherent in the process-heavy system it creates.

Two other recent policy developments also indicate a move towards greater victim responsibilization and stakeholder engagement. The first of these is the *Victims' Right to Review* scheme, introduced by the Coalition in June 2013 to make it easier for victims to seek a review of a Crown Prosecution Service (CPS) decision to discontinue proceedings. The scheme provides an alternative route to seeking a judicial review of a decision, which can be costly and is subject to strict time limits for implementation. For the first six months of the scheme's availability, the number of applications sought averaged 100 a month which was interpreted favourably by some, including Martin Goldman, Chief Crown Prosecutor for Yorkshire and Humberside. He indicated that the scheme allows for a more 'open and transparent' judicial process, providing 'a major step forward in addressing the balance of power towards the victim within the criminal justice system' (Parsons, 2014). However, this commendation was somewhat undermined when discussing the number of reviews sought in his locality. Of the 57,000 cases in Yorkshire where the CPS had decided to discontinue the prosecution, only 34 had been successfully appealed. Goldman's claim that 'the vast majority of victims chose not to exercise their right of review' is not only evidentially unfounded, but appears to be indicating that all victims *were aware* of the availability of the Right to Review and on the basis of this knowledge made informed decisions *not* to pursue this avenue of redress. The responsibility here, it seems, is solely theirs.

Similarly, new measures outlined in the most recent incarnation of the Victims' Code include the victim's entitlement to personally address

DOI: 10.1057/9781137409270.0011

offenders in court to explain how a crime has impacted on them. This is to be done by allowing victims to read out a victim personal statement. Although the statement itself is not new (various incarnations of this existing since 2001) having the *victim* read it out is; in the past, only judges or prosecutors were privy to the contents, the latter having the power to read these out during the trial at the judge's discretion. In terms of quite literally 'hearing victims' voices', this is another incremental means by which the victim as stakeholder has become more visibly (and audibly) prominent in criminal justice process. If this measure assists in meeting additional needs, wants and expectations then it is to be commended. However, previous versions of the victim impact statement appear to have had little notable effect due to victims not being given the opportunity to complete one, statements not reaching the CPS in time, or confusion over the purpose and impact of the statement.

Community and organizational responsibilization

Aside from this top-down responsibilization, notions of community responsibility have been pursued to manage and prevent victimization. These ideas are not new; they are particularly reminiscent of New Labour's ASB agenda, where the 2003 White Paper *Rights and Responsibilities* was grounded in the 'communitarian' values espoused by Etzioni (1993). This rights and responsibilities movement aims to promote moral order by empowering communities, as opposed to relying on formal government control in such areas as crime, the family and education. Indeed, Rogers (2010: 20) uses the analogy of first aid to suggest how training members of the public in community safety skills could facilitate 'co-production' thus enabling the community to respond to conflict and 'Britain's stubbornly high levels of anti-social behaviour'. These community actors are constituted by public service workers, volunteers and householders, who should be involved in community policing to manage low-level disorder. He suggests these actors should be trained in self-protection and restraint, 'reading' situations and conflict resolution. Rogers (2010) acknowledges this could lead to vigilantism, but suggests the training would ensure the skills are operated within the law; quite an assumption.

Further problems abound for this approach, particularly in relation to the triad of offence types we are detailing; although Rogers refers to ASB alone, interconnectedness between ASB and hate crime has been repeatedly outlined in this book. In addition to the statutory sovereign agencies

DOI: 10.1057/9781137409270.0011

doing the 'responsibilizing', Stenson (2005) argues there are other competing levels of crime control, including informal sites of governance such as vigilantism and organized crime, which Rogers (2010) does not take into account. These groups 'have their own agendas of governance, forms of knowledge and expertise deployed to govern and maintain solidarity in and over their own territories and populations' (Stenson, 2005: 267). Consequently, 'there is a problem with social policy rationales that conceptualise both enhanced formal social control and reinvigorated informal social control being developed within a social vacuum' (Casey and Flint, 2007: 77). Stereotypes and prejudices are created by social actors such as the government, employers, local press and community residents (Watt, 2006), which demonstrate that communities are not a social vacuum. Proponents of community responsibilization would see diverse communities as a space for allowing local solutions to be created for local problems; however this if not effective if *no one* acts which is a fundamental flaw of the Big Society ideal.

Effective community responsibilization is hugely problematic in the case of ASB, for example. Victims of ASB are likely to be suffering from targeted, repetitive, escalating abuse within their neighbourhood setting. Therefore the Coalition promising to give more power to communities (Cameron, 2011) and proposals such as Rogers' (2010) are unlikely to positively affect these victims' situation. The problems being faced will not recede overnight, nor will the community itself change in the short term. Just because a new initiative has been announced does not make someone suffering relentless ASB any more confident in reporting or standing up to the perpetrators. In some cases the wider community may not even be aware of the victimization in order to take action. A key problem with Coalition's vision of community responsibilization is that it is characterized by short termism, most likely linked to the relatively short-term periods governments have in power when they can make a difference. The suggestion that communities can be brought together to quickly remedy social ills that have evolved over decades is based on the assumption that everybody in the community wants to 'make a difference' or alter their level of community engagement. This is not to say that such ideas *could not* work, but they would need far greater investment in both financial and human resources to develop communities, as well as a long-term commitment by central government to maintain this support. This notion is supported by Halpern (2001), who indicates it is the importance of social capital, the quality of social networks, that is key to community attempts to control crime. Therefore the politicization of victims in this sense has weakened the position of victims, with the likelihood that successive governments will simply re-fresh and re-brand short-term visions of community responsibilization as a means of responding to victims' needs.

Consequently, it can be argued that victims are seen as the new 'organization' upon which the state relies to conduct their sovereign duties in a range of settings, from investigation (for example, ASB diary data) to justice settings (Garland, 1996). The added bonus of this approach for the government is that it is cost-effective in times of austerity. The reliance on policies that *manage* victims' experiences and the politicization of victims moves beyond the ideas relating to redefinitions of success and failure put forward by Garland (1996), where crime control was deemed to be beyond the state. By producing a raft of measures attempting to redress the failure of the CJS by improving the experience of victimization, it appears the government has reached a point where there is an acceptance that certain policies will not work; akin to a second generation of Martinson's (1974) 'nothing works' pessimism. Perhaps this juncture has been reached as a result of nearly two decades of responsibilization policies, which have not been as welcomed by the public as political elites may have wished. Furthermore, despite the increasingly bureaucratic steps taken to establish various victims' figureheads, champions, spokespeople and representatives, there is an accompanying resignation that victims are still essentially on their own. This approach contradicts the Coalition's symbolic 'helping' the victim rhetoric designed to achieve populist outcomes and instead further indicates how they are focusing on helping the victim's subsequent *experiences*, a far more manageable feat. Whether or not the public will support these administrative avenues remains to be seen. However, in an age of austerity, which appears to have shackled any potentially tangible outcomes, the policies put in place are designed to pacify and placate victims, but leave some victims to fall through the gaps in the system.

Legislating victimization

A core consideration in evolution of this book's critique has been the role and status of victims in light of the forthcoming general election. Retrospective analyses suggest that New Labour established the ASB

DOI: 10.1057/9781137409270.0011

agenda as a means of taking the initiative on law and order *despite* a fall in crime rates becoming more evident towards the end of 1990s (Mooney and Young, 2006). Similar circumstances frame the Coalition's current focus on victimization, indicating a rise in victim consideration at a time when the likelihood of being victimized is potentially at its lowest. The Conservatives may be impeded by their Coalition partners, the Liberal Democrats, if they attempt to progress traditional Conservative law and order policies. Given the power differentials between the parties, there appears to be little chance that this situation will be inverted. As well as being traditionally less vociferous with crime and justice policies (focusing more on addressing issues affecting 'communities'), victims do not feature heavily in Liberal Democrats' rhetoric. Nor are they considered in much depth by the United Kingdom Independence Party (UKIP), an increasingly prominent party promoting nationalist politics whose perspectives on crime and punishment appear more aligned to the Conservatives' right-wing ideologies. Instead, it is the Labour Party which has been most vocal in proposing a codified set of rights for victims. The following section addresses these factors to evaluate developments in how victims are considered against the backdrop of the 2015 general election.

Political posturing

The divide between Coalition political promises and practices for victims was illustrated with the news that since 2010, the Crown Prosecution Service has reduced the number of staff it employs to look after witnesses by more than 50 per cent across England and Wales (McClenaghan and Wright, 2014). These staff form part of the Witness Care Unit service provision, the number of which has also almost halved, from 80 Units in January 2012 to approximately 45 in January 2014. The CPS attributed these reductions to consolidated services and greater police responsibility rather than the impact of Coalition budget cuts to public services (27% in the case of the CPS).

The Witness Charter is the most recent Coalition victim-focused set of guidelines, published in December 2013. This outlines 'standards of care' for witnesses which include being treated with dignity and respect at all times; having a main point of contact throughout the process; being needs assessed (particularly for categorization as a 'vulnerable or intimidated' witness); reasonable measures being taken regarding witnesses'

DOI: 10.1057/9781137409270.0011

availability to attend court and safety once there; being able to avail of pre-trial visits; being kept informed of details, progress and outcomes; being able to claim expenses; and having the right to complain if dissatisfied with the service provided (Ministry of Justice, 2013a). Special measures are available for witnesses, some of whom may be victims, deemed to be 'vulnerable' (under 18 years old, or having a mental, physical or learning disability) or 'intimidated' (victims of sexual offences or human trafficking, or witness to a gun or knife offence) (Ministry of Justice, 2013a). The rise in political concern for 'vulnerable' victims has prioritized this category generally. Comments regarding the cuts to witness services made by Adam Pemberton, Assistant Chief Executive of Victim Support, unsurprisingly focused on 'vulnerable and intimidated witnesses who arrive at court without any provision having been made for their needs' (McClenaghan and Wright, 2014). Not all victims are included within this rhetoric of vulnerability, but for those who are emerging as a dominant cohort within this discourse – most notably female victims of male predatory sexual abuse, sexual grooming and enforced prostitution – the identity factors they embody usefully align to 'ideal victim' characteristics.

Preceding the Witness Charter was the updated Code of Practice for Victims of Crime, published in October 2013 (Ministry of Justice, 2013). Whilst not constituting a set of rights, the Code sets out various services and provisions to victims who have directly experienced crime, have reported this to the police and been affected by their victimization. The statutory obligations, therefore, concern the service providers. The consultation process undertaken for this most recent incarnation of the Code was facilitated whilst Helen Grant MP was Victims' Minister who, in the consultation document, details her extensive experience working with victims of domestic abuse and hate crime. This experience, and the extensive consultation undertaken with victims' groups, informed the proposals to put in place enhanced services for victims who fall into one or more categories of being a victim of a serious crime, being a persistently targeted victim and being a vulnerable and intimidated victim. A list of crime types which may warrant an enhanced level of service is outlined in the Code, but the decision as to whether or not a particular victim qualifies ultimately rests with the relevant service provider (such as the CPS, the courts service, PCCs, Witness Care Units). Although hate crime is included in this categorization for enhanced service provision, given the aforementioned reasons why victims may choose not to

DOI: 10.1057/9781137409270.0011

engage with the CJS, this either makes them responsible for their exclusion, or forces them down a criminal justice route. Victims of ASB are excluded altogether despite potentially incurring persistent and targeted victimization.

Labour has also sought to capitalize on the victims' rights discussion as a general election tactic. In 2014, Keir Starmer, chief prosecutor from 2008 until 2013, began advising Labour on the possible implementation of legal changes in this area if they were to be elected. Starmer has been particularly vocal regarding changes to the questioning of rape and sexual abuse victims during trials. Several high-profile cases were reported in 2013 whereby the treatment of victims of serious crimes made headline news for tragic reasons. Examples include violinist Frances Andrade, who killed herself after giving evidence against former teacher Michael Brewer, who was later found guilty of indecently assaulting her. However, it was the ways in which child victims of paedophile and sexual exploitation rings in Oxfordshire were cross-examined by barristers which caused most distress and informed Starmer's suggestions for change. However, on a more sceptical note, Mr Starmer's advisory endeavours – and specific focus on victims of high-profile, emotive cases – may well be linked to his political aspirations affiliated to the Labour Party. His victims' taskforce to promote various changes includes murdered teenager Stephen Lawrence's mother, Labour peer Baroness Lawrence of Clarendon, whose high public and media profile stands her in good stead to promote victims' voices. Starmer's proposals have also been supported by shadow justice secretary Sadiq Khan on the basis that they would increase public confidence in the criminal justice system where currently confusion and inadequacy abound, largely as a result of the variety of Codes and Charters across various government agencies (BBC News, 2014).

Political prioritizing of specific victim types has also been emulated by Labour through their proposal to create a National Women's Champion to address domestic and sexual violence if they were to be elected in 2015 (Merrick and Dugan, 2013). However, with the lack of tangible, long-term outcomes from previous figureheads this policy appears at best populist and at worst a misuse of resources. In any case, Labour's chance of winning may be dependent upon on UKIP being able to split the right-wing vote (Cohen, 2014). Following a good showing during the May 2013 elections, UKIP has put the pressure on David Cameron to take a more hard-line approach on topics such as immigration, involvement with

DOI: 10.1057/9781137409270.0011

Europe and crime. Their gradual rise in popularity has led commentators to suggest that UKIP may make it difficult for the Conservatives to win outright in the 2015 general election in what has been deemed a 'four-party race' (Martin, 2014). With opinion polls demonstrating that UKIP has been commanding up to 16 per cent of the vote, they may well be in a position to form a coalition with the Conservatives (Mason, 2013). Although UKIP demonstrates a limited policy remit, with regards to law and order, they generally advocate no policing cuts; life sentences to mean 'life'; no votes for prisoners; withdrawal from the European Union; the prevention of foreign criminals entering the UK; cessation of the European arrest warrant; the removal of the UK from the European Court of Human Rights' jurisdiction. If crime victims were to feature later into their political campaign, UKIP would need to address from where the money for victims' services would arise, given their intense focus on retributive and frontline policing. Their concern for tougher sentencing may not sit well with the electorate either. Public views on sentencing tend to vary considerably between perception and practice. For example, findings from research suggesting that six out of ten people believed sentences to be too lenient (Roberts and Hough, 2005) can be juxtaposed with findings from research showing that, when presented with all the facts of a case, members of the public chose similar or more lenient sentences to those which had been delivered (Sentencing Advisory Panel, 2010).

At present, crime victims do not appear to be on the Liberal Democrats and UKIP's radars (although following the severe flooding in parts of rural England in January 2014, UKIP leader Nigel Farage has had plenty to say about assisting flood victims). As well as proposing victims' rights, Labour has also been raising concerns about the safety risks to the public as a result of privatization plans involving G4S and Serco. Criminal justice is one of the key areas targeted as part of the government's £81 billion spending cuts to address the £155 billion deficit (Howard League for Penal Reform, 2009; Office for Budget Responsibility, 2010). Where previously over £22 billion was made available for the justice sector alone, current austerity measures have led the Coalition to offset cuts with the tendering out of CJS services to for-profit companies. Plans outlined by Justice Minister Chris Grayling have included privatizing the enforcement of fines and compensation set by the criminal courts as part of the Crime and Courts Act 2013. This Act allows for the judicial functions of fines officers to be outsourced to firms such as Capita, Serco

DOI: 10.1057/9781137409270.0011

and G4S who will then be entrusted with decisions such as whether money should be deducted from offenders' benefits or directly from their earnings, as well as varying the duration or amount of instalments they must pay. It is possible that the poorly regulated private bailiffs will be tasked with collecting payments from criminals, whilst victims of crime who are owed compensation for personal injury, loss or damage resulting from an offence will have their personal data handed to debt collectors potentially without their consent.

Conclusion and recommendations

An unprecedented level of visibility is currently afforded to addressing victimization in the criminal justice system, with victims – past, present and potential – occupying a central role in this rhetoric. When things appear too good to be true, they usually are; thus, a moral responsibility befalls scholars to question such seemingly 'public-spirited' developments to critically assess their impact on the individual and society. For a start, it appears that not all victims (or experiences of victimization) are equal. Second, it remains the case that victim policy is being designed around fitting victims into the existing format; one which seeks a specific form of *justice* for *criminal* infractions, via a linear *system* not initially designed with victims' needs or wants in mind. Third, a significant level of political rhetoric infers claims to be acting in the interests of a punitively minded public whilst invoking images of 'vulnerable' victims to validate such positions. This, we contend, amounts to progressing retributive penal policies through the back door.

In light of the factors discussed in this book, we suggest that there is a need to move victimological analyses forward in several respects, such as considering victimization from a perspective of similarity rather than difference. With regards to ASB and hate crime, thinking up catchy acronyms, or enhancing the criminalization of existing offences, is unlikely to reduce or prevent targeted victimization. Resources would be better deployed in trying to address the social and economic factors *underpinning* such prejudice to eliminate victimization in the first place (not unlike the approach taken in another current government policy entitled End Violence Against Women).

Within the victimological domain, changes in approach are required to match the rise in administrating victimization with critical analyses of the processes and implications this brings, including among the wider victim cohort. Whilst it would be useful to term our investigation 'administrative victimology', there is a danger that comparisons may be made to 'administrative criminology', heavily critiqued on the basis of its narrow conceptualization of what constitutes crime and failure to adequately address relevant causes. A critical victimological focus on the politically sanctioned imposition of victim management offers a means to uncover the nature and impact on victims, their advocates, as well as other victim-oriented stakeholders and figureheads. If processes of segregation and hierarchization continue to divide victims along demarcated, prioritized and responsibilized lines as suggested, then a very different politics of victimization may evolve which would the most vulnerable in society with little or no representation.

There is also scope to broaden this investigation out to encompass areas not addressed in the present analysis, such as victims' access to, or involvement in, restorative justice (which links to Community Remedy in ASB legislation), the importance of risk in determining victim trajectories and outcomes, and the changing nature of vulnerability in light of the growing focus on the diverse nature of sexual abuse victims. Returning to the fact that the Coalition initially failed to consider victims in their programme for government, paying closer attention to how victims are incorporated in light of other factors may shed some light on how relevant victims' issues really are to those tasked with legislating for them.

Summary of key points

▸ Hierarchies of victimization have emerged which may prioritize victims according to newly demarcated forms of victim identity.
▸ Victimization processes have been subject to enhanced levels of political administration, indicating a growing bureaucratic approach to interacting with victims.
▸ Victimological enquiry is needed to see the wider nature and impact of emerging forms of politicized victimization on the individual and society.

DOI: 10.1057/9781137409270.0011

References

ACPO (2010) *Hate Crime Data for 2010.* Available at: http://www.report-it.org.uk/files/acpo_hate_crime_data_for2010.pdf

Albertson, K., Albertson, K. Fox, C. and Ellingworth, D. (2013) 'Economic Values and Evidence: Evaluating Criminal Justice Policy' in M. Cowburn, M. Duggan, A. Robinson and P. Senior (eds) *Values in Criminology and Community Justice.* Bristol: The Policy Press.

Amir, M. (1971) *Patterns in Forcible Rape.* Chicago: University of Chicago Press.

Aradau, C. (2004) 'The Perverse Politics of Four-Letter Words: Risk and Pity in the Securitisation of Human Trafficking', *Millennium – Journal of International Studies*, 33(2): 251–278.

Ashe, J., Campbell, R., Childs, S. and Evans, E. (2010) '"Stand by your Man": Women's Political Recruitment at the 2010 General Election', *British Politics*, 5(40): 455–480.

Bache, I. (2003) 'Not Everything That Matters Is Measurable and Not Everything That Is Measurable Matters: How and Why Local Education Authorities "Fail"', *Local Government Studies*, 29(4): 76–94.

Bannister, J. and Kearns, A. (2009) 'Tolerance, Respect and Civility Amid Changing Cities' in Millie, A. (ed.) *Securing Respect: Behavioural Expectations and Anti-Social Behaviour in the UK.* Bristol: Policy Press.

Bannister, J. and Scott, S. (2000) Assessing the Cost-Effectiveness of Measures to Deal with Anti-Social Neighbour Behaviour. Discussion Paper No. 1, Department of Urban Studies University of Glasgow.

112

BBC News (2009) Sara Payne New Victims' Champion. http://news.bbc. co.uk/1/hi/uk/7850785.stm

BBC News (2011) MPs Expenses: Repayments Totalled £1.46m. Available at: http://www.bbc.co.uk/news/uk-politics-13033783 Last Accessed: February 2014.

BBC News (2012) UK Economy in Double Dip Recession. Available at: http://www.bbc.co.uk/news/business-17836624 Last Accessed: February 2014.

BBC News (2014) Keir Starmer Heads Labour's Victim Treatment Review. Available at: http://www.bbc.co.uk/news/uk-politics-25528966 Last Accessed: February 2014.

BBC News (2014a) 'Plebgate Affair: Met PC Admits Misconduct. Available at: http://www.bbc.co.uk/news/uk-25682652 Last Accessed: February 2014.

Becker, H. (1967) 'Whose Side Are We on?' *Social Problems*, 14(3): 239–247.

Betham, J. (1798/1996) *An Introduction to the Principles of Morals and Legislation*, J. H. Burns and H. L. A. Hart (eds). Oxford: Clarendon Press.

Big Brother Watch (2012) *A Legacy of Suspicion: How RIPA Has Been Used by Local Authorities and Public Bodies.* London: Big Brother Watch. http://www.bigbrotherwatch.org.uk/files/ripa/RIPA_Aug12_final.pdf Last Accessed: February 2014.

Blondel, J. and M. Cotta (1996) 'Conclusions' in J. Blondel and M. Cotta (eds) *Party and Government. An Inquiry into the Relationship between Governments and Supporting Parties in Liberal Democracies.* London: Palgrave Macmillan.

Blondel, J. and M. Cotta (eds) (2000) *The Nature of Party Government: A Comparative European Perspective.* London: Palgrave Macmillan.

Boffey, D. and Helm, T. (2012) Battered Coalition Partners Begin to Doubt Strategy of Compromise. *The Guardian.* Available at: http://www.theguardian.com/politics/2012/may/05/nick-clegg-david-cameron-election Last Accessed: February 2014.

Bowcott, O. (2012) Twitter Joke Ruling Hailed as Victory for Free Speech. *The Guardian.* Available at: http://www.theguardian.com/law/2012/jul/27/twitter-joke-victory-free-speech Last Accessed: February 2014.

Brand, S. and Price, R. (2000) *The Economic and Social Costs of Crime.* Home Office Research Study 217. Available at: http://webarchive.

DOI: 10.1057/9781137409270.0012

nationalarchives.gov.uk/20110218135832/rds.homeoffice.gov.uk/rds/
pdfs/hors217.pdf

Brown, K. J. (2013) 'The Developing Habitus of the Anti-Social Behaviour Practitioner: From Expansion in Years of Plenty to Surviving the Age of Austerity', *Journal of Law and Society*, 40(3): 375–402.

Budd, T. and Sims, L. (2001) *Anti-Social Behaviour and Disorder: Findings from the 2000 British Crime Survey: Findings 145*. London: Home Office.

Cabinet Office (2010) *The Coalition: Our Programme for Government*. London Cabinet Office, Whitehall: London. www.hmg.gov.uk/programmeforgovernment Last Accessed: February 2014.

Cameron, D. (2011) *Speech on Big Society*, made in London, 14 February. Available at: http://www.number10.gov.uk/news/pms-speech-on-big-society/ Last Accessed: February 2014.

Card, R. and Ward, R. (1998) *The Crime and Disorder Act 1998 – A Practitioner's Guide*. Bristol: Jordan's.

Carrabine, E., Cox, P., Lee, M., Plummer, K., South, N. and Turton, J. (2009) *Criminology: A Sociological Introduction* (2nd edn). London: Routledge.

Casey, L. (2011) *Review into the Needs of Families Bereaved by Homicide*. Available at: http://www.justice.gov.uk/downloads/news/press-releases/victims-com/review-needs-of-families-bereaved-by-homicide.pdf Last Accessed: February 2014.

Casey, R. and Flint, J. (2007) 'Active Citizenship in the Governance of Anti-Social Behaviour in the UK: Exploring the Non-Reporting of Incidents', *People, Place and Policy Online*, 1(2): 69–79.

Census (2011) Available at: http://www.ons.gov.uk/ons/rel/census/2011-census/key-statistics-for-local-authorities-in-england-and-wales/rpt-religion.html

Chakraborti, N. (2010) 'Future Developments for Hate Crime Thinking: Who, What and Why?' in Chakraborti, N. (ed.) *Hate Crime: Concepts, Policy, Future Directions*. Cullompton: Willan.

Christie, N. (1977) 'Conflicts as Property', *British Journal of Criminology*, 17(1): 1–15.

Christie, N. (1986) 'The Ideal Victim' in E. Fattah (ed.) *From Crime Policy to Victim Policy*. Basingstoke: Palgrave Macmillan.

Clarke, A., Williams, K., Wydall, S., Gray, P., Liddle, M. and Smith, A. (2011) *Describing and Assessing Interventions to Address Anti-Social Behaviour*. Home Office Research Report 51. London: Home Office.

DOI: 10.1057/9781137409270.0012

Cohen, L. E. and Felson, M. (1979) 'Social Change and Crime Rate Trends: A Routine Activities Approach', *American Sociological Review*, 44: 588–608.

Cohen, N. (2014) UKIP's Rise Threatens the Left as Well as the Right. *The Guardian*. Available at: http://www.theguardian.com/commentisfree/2014/feb/01/ukip-nigel-farage-rise-labour-no-good Last Accessed: February 2014.

Cohen, S. (1972) *Folk Devils and Moral Panics*. London: Routledge.

Cohen, S. (1979) 'The Punitive City: Notes on the Dispersal of Social Control', *Contemporary Crises*, 3(4): 341–363.

Cohen, S. (1985) *Visions of Social Control*. Cambridge: Polity Press.

Conservative Party (2010) *Invitation to Join the Government of Britain: The Conservative Manifesto 2010*. London: Conservative Party.

Cook, K. and Jones, H. (2007) 'Surviving Victimhood: The Impact of Feminist Campaigns' in S. Walklate (ed.) *The Handbook of Victims and Victimology*. Cullompton: Willan.

CPS (2012) *Hate Crime and Crimes against Older People Report 2010–2011*. Available at: http://www.cps.gov.uk/publications/docs/cps_hate_crime_report_2011.pdf

Crawford, A. (1997) *The Local Governance of Crime: Appeals to Community and Partnerships*. Clarendon Press: Oxford.

Currie, E. (2010) 'Plain Left Realism: An Appreciation, and Some Thoughts for the Future', *Crime, Law and Social Change*, 54: 111–124.

Davies, P. (2007) 'Criminal (in)Justice for Victims?' in P. Davies, P. Francis, and C. Greer (eds) *Victims, Crime and Society*. London: Sage.

Deans, M. (2010) *Governmentality: Power and Rule in Modern Society*. London: Sage.

DeKeserdy, W. and Schwartz, M. (1991) 'British and US Left Realism: A Critical Comparison', *International Journal of Offender Therapy and Comparative Criminology*, 35L 248–262.

Dick, S. (2008) *Homophobic Hate Crime: The Gay British Crime Survey*. Stonewall. Available at: http://www.stonewall.org.uk/documents/homophobic_hate_crime__final_report.pdf

Downes, D. and Rock, P. (2011) *Understanding Deviance* (6th edn). Oxford: Oxford University Press.

Duffy, B., Wake, R., Burrows, T. and Bremner P. (2008) *Closing the Gap: Crime and Public Perceptions*. London: Ipsos MORI

Duggan, M. (2012) 'Using Victims' Voices to Prevent Violence Against Women: A Critique', *British Journal of Community Justice*, 10(2): 25–38.

DOI: 10.1057/9781137409270.0012

Duggan, M. (2013) 'Working with Victims: Values and Validations' in M. Cowburn, M. Duggan, A. Robinson and P. Senior (eds) *The Values of Criminology and Community Justice*. Bristol: The Policy Press.

Duggan, M. (2014) 'Working with Lesbian, Gay, Bisexual and Transgender Communities to Shape Hate Crime Policy' in N. Chakraborti and J. Garland (eds) *Responding to Hate Crime: The Case for Connecting Policy and Research*. Bristol: The Policy Press.

Duggan, M. and Heap. V. (2013) 'Victims as Vote-Winners? Exploring the Antisocial Behaviour/Hate Crime Nexus', *Criminal Justice Matters*, 94(1): 24–25.

Edwards, A. (2012) 'Police and Crime Commissioners', *Criminal Law Review*, 11: 821–823.

Elias, N. (1994) *The Civilizing Process* (revised edn). Oxford: Blackwell.

Elias, R. (1986) *The Politics of Victimisation*. New York: Oxford University Press.

Elias, R. (1990) 'Which Victim Movement: The Politics of Victim Policy' in A. Lurigio (ed.) *Victims of Crime*, Sage Publications: Newbury Park, CA.

Elias, R. (1993) *Victims Still*, Sage Publications: Newbury Park, CA.

Etzioni, A. (1993) *The Spirit of Community: Rights, Responsibilities and the Communitarian Agenda*. London: Fontana Press.

Everyday Sexism Project (2014) Available at: http://everydaysexism.com/ Last Accessed: February 2014.

Farrall, S. and Hay, C. (2010) 'Not So Tough on Crime? Why Weren't the Thatcher Governments More Radical in Reforming the Criminal Justice System?' *British Journal of Criminology* 50: 550–569.

Financial Times (2010) UK Unveils Dramatic Austerity Measures. Available at: http://www.ft.com/cms/s/0/53fe06e2-dc98-11df-84f5 00144feabdc0.html#axzz2pRYq7Uo0 Last Accessed: February 2014.

Financial Times (2013) George Osborne Takes EU to Court over Bank Bonus Cap. Available at: http://www.ft.com/cms/s/0/0f54735a-25f6-11e3-8ef6-00144feab7de.html#axzz2pXZeK2Ly Last Accessed: February 2014.

Flint, J. (2006) 'Introduction' in Flint, J. (ed.) *Housing, Urban Governance and Anti-Social Behaviour*. Bristol: Policy Press.

Flint, J. and Nixon, J. (2006) 'Governing Neighbours: Anti-Social Behaviour Orders and New Forms of Regulating Conduct in the UK', *Urban Studies*, 43(5): 939–955.

DOI: 10.1057/9781137409270.0012

Foucault, M. (1975) *Discipline and Punish: The Birth of the Prison*. New York: Random House.

Foucault, M. (1979) *The History of Sexuality, vol. 1. An Introduction.* London: Allen.

Foucault, M. (1991) 'Governmentality' in G. Burchell, C. Gordon and P. Miller (eds) *The Foucault Effect: Studies in Governmentality*. Hemel Hempstead: Harvester Wheatsheaf.

Franklyn, R. (2012) *Satisfaction and Willingness to Engage with the Criminal Justice System: Findings from the Witness and Victim Experience Survey, 2009–10.* Ministry of Justice Research Series 1/12. London: Ministry of Justice.

Furedi, F. (1998) 'New Britain – A Nation of Victims', *Society*, February 1998.

Garland, D. (1996) 'The Limits of the Sovereign State: Strategies of Crime Control in Contemporary Society', *British Journal of Criminology*, 36(4): 445–471.

Garland, D. (2001) *The Culture of Control*. Oxford: Oxford University Press.

Garland, J. (2010) 'The Victimisation of Goths and the Boundaries of Hate Crime' in Chakraborti, N. (ed.) *Hate Crime: Concepts, Policy, Future Directions*. Cullompton: Willan.

Garland, J. and Chakraborti, N. (2009) *Hate Crime: Impact, Causes, and Consequences*. London: Sage.

Garland, D. and Sparks, R. (2000) 'Criminology, Social Theory and the Challenge of Our Times' in D. Garland and R. Sparks (eds) *Criminology and Social Theory*. Oxford: Oxford University Press.

Gilmore, M. (2012) 'Poll Reflects Public Concerns About Police and Crime Commissioners', *The RUSI Journal*, 157(5): 12–15.

Godfrey, B. Cox, D., and Farrall, S. (2007) *Criminal Lives: Family Life, Employment and Offending*. Clarendon Series in Criminology. Oxford: Oxford University Press.

Great Britain, Parliament, House of Lords (2013) *Anti-Social Behaviour, Crime and Policing Bill*. London: The Stationary Office. Bill 7 (2013–14).

Great Britain, Parliament, House of Lords (2013a) *Anti-Social Behaviour, Crime and Policing Bill*, Fourth Marshalled List of Amendments to be Moved in Committee, Instruction of 5th November 2013 [online]. London: The Stationary Office. Available at: http://www.publications. parliament.uk/pa/bills/lbill/2013–2014/0052/amend/ml052-IV.htm Last Accessed: February 2014.

DOI: 10.1057/9781137409270.0012

Green, D. (2006) We're (Nearly) All Victims Now! How Political Correctness Is Undermining Our Liberal Culture. Civitas: Institute for the Study of Civil Society: London Available at: http://www.civitas.org.uk/pdf/Victims.pdf

Green, S. (2007) 'Crime, Victimisation and Vulnerability' in S. Walklate (ed.) *Handbook of Victims and Victimology*. Collumpton: Willan.

Hall, M. (2010) *Victims and Policy Making*. Abingdon: Willan.

Hall, N. (2013) *Hate Crime*. Taylor & Francis.

Halpern, D. (2001) 'Moral Values, Social Trust and Inequality – Can Values Explain Crime?' *British Journal of Criminology*, 41(2): 236–251.

Hamilton-Smith, N. (2004) *The Reducing Burglary Initiative: Design, Development and Delivery*. Home Office Research Study 287. London: Home Office.

Harding, R. (1994) 'Victimisation, Moral Panics, and the Distortion of Criminal Justice Policy', *Current Issues in Criminal Justice*, 6: 27–42.

Heap, V. (2010) Understanding Public Perceptions of Anti-Social Behaviour: Problems and Policy Responses. PhD Dissertation. University of Huddersfield.

Heilbroner, R. (1985) *The Nature and Logic of Capitalism*. New York: W. W. Norton.

Her Majesty's Inspectorate of Constabulary (2010) *Anti-Social Behaviour: Stop the Rot*. London: HMIC.

HL Debate (2013–14) 8 January 2014 c1499. [online] Available at: http://www.publications.parliament.uk/pa/ld201314/ldhansrd/text/140108-0001.htm#14010845000398 Last Accessed: February 2014.

HM Government (2010) *The Coalition: Our Programme for Government*. London: Cabinet Office. Available at: http://www.cabinetoffice.gov.uk/media/409088/pfg_coalition.pdf Last Accessed: February 2014.

HM Government (March 2012) *Challenge It, Report It, Stop It: The Government's Plan to Tackle Hate Crime*. Available at https://www.gov.uk/government/publications/the-coalition-documentation

HM Government (2013) *Anti-Social Behaviour Order Statistics: England and Wales 2012*. Available at: https://www.gov.uk/government/publications/anti-social-behaviour-order-statistics-england-and-wales-2012 Last accessed: March 2014.

DOI: 10.1057/9781137409270.0012

HM Government (2013a) Damian Green's Speech to the Association of PCCs. Available at: https://www.gov.uk/government/speeches/damian-greens-speech-to-the-association-of-pccs Last Accessed: February 2014.

HM Government (2013b) Victims Put First in the Criminal Justice System. Available at: https://www.gov.uk/government/news/victims-put-first-in-the-criminal-justice-system Last Accessed: February 2014.

HM Government (2014) Helping and Supporting Victims of Crime https://www.gov.uk/government/policies/helping-and-supporting-victims-of-crime

HM Government (2014a) More Than £16million to Help Victims Rebuild Their Lives. Available at: https://www.gov.uk/government/news/more-than-16-million-to-help-victims-rebuild-their-lives Last Accessed: March 2014.

HM Treasury (2009) *Securing Recovery: Growth and Opportunity*. Pre-Budget Report 2009. London: Crown Copyright.

HM Treasury (2010) *Spending Review 2010*. London: Crown Copyright.

HM Treasury (2013) *Spending Round 2013*. London: Crown Copyright.

Home Office (1999) *Crime and Disorder Act: Guidance on Anti-Social Behaviour Orders*. London: Home Office.

Home Office (2011) Available at: http://services.parliament.uk/bills/2010–11/policereformandsocialresponsibility.html accessed 6/1/14. Last Accessed: February 2014.

Home Office (2011a) *Police and Crime Commissioners: Have You Got What It Takes?* London: Home Office.

Home Office (2012) *Putting Victims First: More Effective Responses to Anti-Social Behaviour*. London: Home Office.

Home Office (2013) *Reform of Anti-Social Behaviour Powers: Draft Guidance for Frontline Professionals*. London: Home Office.

House of Commons Library (2013) *Police Service Strength*. Standard Note 00634. London: House of Commons Library.

Hoyle, C. (2007) 'Feminism, Victimology and Domestic Violence' in S. Walklate (ed.) *The Handbook of Victims and Victimology*. Cullompton: Willan.

Iganski, P. (2002) 'Hate Crimes Hurt More, but Should They Be More Harshly Punished?' in P. Iganski (ed.) *The Hate Debate*. London: Profile.

DOI: 10.1057/9781137409270.0012

Independent Police Commission (2013) *Policing for a Better Britain.* Essex: Lord Stevens of Kirkwhelpington QPM.

Jacobs, J. and Potter, K. (1998) *Hate Crimes: Criminal Law and Identity Politics.* New York, NY: Oxford University Press.

Jordan, J. (2001) 'Worlds Apart? Women, Rape and the Reporting Process', *British Journal of Criminology,* 41(4): 679–706.

Joseph Rowntree Foundation (2014) Tough on People in Poverty – New Report Shows Public's Hardening Attitudes to Welfare. Available at: http://www.jrf.org.uk/media-centre/tough-attitudes-poverty Last accessed: April 2014.

Kearon, T. and Godfrey, B. (2007) 'Setting the Scene: A Question of History' in S. Walklate (ed.) *The Handbook of Victims and Victimology.* Cullompton: Willan.

Kelly, L. (1988) *Surviving Sexual Violence.* London: Wiley Blackwell.

Kemshall, H., Wood, J., Westwood, S., Stout, B., Wilkinson, B., Kelly G. and Mackenzie, G. (2010) *Child Sex Offender Review (CSOR) Public Disclosure Pilots: A Process Evaluation* (2nd edn). Research Report 32. London: Home Office.

Kennedy, M. (2013) Mary Beard is the Latest Woman to Be Sent a Bomb Threat on Twitter. *The Guardian.* Available at: http://www.theguardian.com/technology/2013/aug/04/mary-beard-bomb-threat-twitter Last Accessed: February 2014.

Krauthammer, C. (1993) Defining Deviancy Up. *The New Republic,* 22 November.

Lammy, D. (2014) Mark Duggan Inquest: Questions Must Be Answered before Police and Community Relations Can Heal. *The Guardian.* Available at: http://www.theguardian.com/commentisfree/2014/jan/08/mark-duggan-inquest-serious-questions-police-relations Last Accessed: February 2014.

Law Commission (2013) *Hate Crime: The Case for Extending the Existing Offences.* Consultation Paper No 213. Available at: http://lawcommission.justice.gov.uk/docs/cp213_hate_crime_amended.pdf

Laxminarayan, M., Bosmans, M., Porter, R. and Sosa, L. (2013) 'Victim Satisfaction with Criminal Justice: A Systematic Review', *Victims and Offenders,* 8: 119–147.

Lea, J. (2010) 'Left Realism, Community and State-Building', *Crime, Law and Social Change,* 54: 141–158.

DOI: 10.1057/9781137409270.0012

Lea, J. and Young, J. (1984) *What Is to Be Done about Law and Order? – Crisis in the Eighties*. Harmondsworth: Penguin.

Lemke, T. (2001) ' "The Birth of Bio-Politics" – Michel Foucault's Lecture at the Collège de France on Neo-Liberal Governmentality', *Economy & Society*, 30(2): 190–207.

Liberal Democrats (2010) *Liberal Democrat Manifesto 2010: Change That Works for You*. London: Liberal Democrats.

Lombroso, C. (1876/2006) *Criminal Man* (M. Gibson & N. H. Rafter trans.) Durham, NC: Duke University Press.

Madlingozi, T. (2007) 'Good Victims, Bad Victims: Apartheid's Beneficiaries, Victims and the Struggle for Social Justice' in W. Le Roux and K. van Marle (eds) *Law, Memory and the Legacy of Apartheid*. Pretoria: Pretoria University Press.

Maguire, M. and Pointing, J. (eds.) (1988) *Victims of Crime: A New Deal?* Michigan: Open University Press.

Martin, I. (2014) The Rise of UKIP and the Lib Dems being Rubbish Are Keeping Ed Miliband in a Job. *The Telegraph*. Available at: http://blogs.telegraph.co.uk/news/iainmartin1/100256031/the-rise-of-ukip-and-the-lib-dems-being-rubbish-are-keeping-ed-miliband-in-a-job/ Last Accessed: February 2014.

Martinson, R. (1974) 'What Works? Questions and Answer about Prison Reform', *The Public Interest*, 35: 22–54.

Mason, R. (2013) UKIP Could Be in 2015 Coalition Government. *The Telegraph*. Available at: http://www.telegraph.co.uk/news/politics/ukip/9784758/Ukip-could-be-in-2015-Coalition-Government.html Last Accessed: February 2014.

Mason-Bish, H. (2010) 'Future Challenges for Hate Crime Policy: Lessons from the Past' in Chakraborti, N. (ed.) *Hate Crime: Concepts, Policy, Future Directions*. Cullompton: Willan.

Mawby, R. and Walklate, S. (1994) *Critical Victimology*. London: Sage.

May, T. (2010) Speech at the Coin Street Community Centre, London 28 July, Available at: https://www.gov.uk/government/speeches/crime-home-secretarys-speech-on-moving-beyond-the-asbo-28-july-2010 Last Accessed: February 2014.

Mayer, I., Edelenbos, J. and Monnikhof, R. (2005) 'Interactive Policy Development: Undermining or Sustaining Democracy?' *Public Administration*, 83(1): 179–199.

DOI: 10.1057/9781137409270.0012

Mayhew, P. and Hough, M. (1988) 'The British Crime Survey: Origins and Impact' in M. Maguire and J. Pointing (eds) *Victims of Crime: A New Deal?* Milton Keynes: Open University Press.

McClenaghan, M. and Wright, O. (2014) Revealed: Hoa the CPS Betrays Victims of Crime – Numbers of Witness Protection Staff Falls by 57% in Just Three Years. *The Independent.* Available at: http://www.independent.co.uk/news/uk/politics/revealed-how-the-cps-betrays-victims-of-crime--numbers-of-staff-assigned-to-look-after-witnesses-falls-by-57-in-just-three-years-9150172.html Last Accessed: February 2014.

Mellor, A. (2013) 'A Code that is not being followed is of little value' Ombudsman highlights poor awareness of Code that protects victims of crime as Ministry of Justice launch a consultation on changes'. Parliamentary and Health Ombudsman Website. Available at: http://www.ombudsman.org.uk/about-us/news-centre/press-releases/2013/a-code-that-is-not-being-followed-is-of-little-value-ombudsman-highlights-poor-awareness-of-code-that-protects-victims-of-crime-as-ministry-of-justice-launch-a-consultation-on-changes Last Accessed: February 2014.

Mendelsohn, B. (1947) New Biopsychosocial Horizons: Victimology. Paper presented to the Psychiatric Society of Bucharest, Coltzea State Hospital, Hungary.

Merrick, J. and Dugan, E. (2013) Enough! Labour Vows Action on Rape and Abuse as Shadow Home Secretary announces 'Women's Champion' to Tackle Domestic and Sexual Violence. *The Independent.* Available at: http://www.independent.co.uk/news/uk/politics/enough-labour-vows-action-on-rape-and-abuse-as-shadow-home-secretary-announces-womens-champion-to-tackle-domestic-and-sexual-violence-8831834.html Last Accessed: February 2014.

Miers, D. (1978) *The Politicisation of the Victim.* Abingdon: Professional Books.

Miers, D. (1990) 'Positivist Victimology: A Critique', *International Review of Victimology*, 1(3): 219–230.

Ministry of Justice (2007) *Penal Policy: A Background Paper.* London: Ministry of Justice.

Ministry of Justice (2013) *Code of Practice for Victims of Crime.*

Ministry of Justice (2013a) *The Witness Charter: Standards of Care for Witnesses in the Criminal Justice System.*

DOI: 10.1057/9781137409270.0012

Ministry of Justice (MoJ) (2012) *Getting It Right for Victims and Witnesses.* Consultation Paper CP3/2012, MoJ, London, January 2012. Available at: www.justice.gov.uk/downloads/consultations/getting-it-right-for-victims-and-witnesses.pdf. Last Accessed: February 2014.

Mooney, J. and Young, J. (2006) 'The Decline in Crime and the Rise of Anti-Social Behaviour', *Probation Journal*, 53(4): 397–407.

Morris, N. (2009) 'Victims' Champion Seeks Justice Reform', *The Independent*. Friday 06 November 2009. Available at: http://www.independent.co.uk/news/uk/home-news/victims-champion-seeks-justice-reform-1815740.html

Morris, N. (2012) Crime Prevention Cash Cut by £35m since 2010. *The Independent*. Available at: http://www.independent.co.uk/news/uk/crime/crime-prevention-cash-cut-by-35m-since-2010–8231607.html Last Accessed: February 2014.

Moynihan, D. P. (1993) 'Defining Deviancy Down', *American Scholar*, 62(Winter): 17–30.

NatCen Social Research (2014) http://www.natcen.ac.uk/study/public-attitudes-to-poverty-and-welfare LINK BROKEN, see (http://www.jrf.org.uk/media-centre/tough-attitudes-poverty) Last Accessed: February 2014.

National Housing Federation (2014) Bedroom Tax. Available at: http://www.housing.org.uk/policy/welfare-reform/bedroom-tax Last Accessed: February 2014.

Newburn, T. and Stanko, B. (1994) 'When Men Are Victims: The Failure of Victimology' in T. Newburn and B. Stanko (eds) *Just Boys Doing Business?* London: Routledge.

Nixon, J., Blandy, S., Hunter, C., Reeve, K. and Jones, A. (2003) *Tackling Anti-Social Behaviour in Mixed Tenure Areas.* London: ODPM.

Office for National Statistics (2013) *Crime in England and Wales, Year Ending March 2013.* London: Crown Copyright.

Office for National Statistics (2014) *Crime Statistics, period ending December 2013.* Available at: http://www.ons.gov.uk/ons/rel/crime-stats/crime-statistics/period-ending-december-2013/index.html

Owen, P. (2013) Every Coalition U-Turn: The List in Full. *The Guardian.* Available at: http://www.theguardian.com/politics/2012/may/31/coalition-u-turns-full-list Last Accessed: February 2014.

Parsons, R. (2014) Exclusive: Victims of Crime Given Hope as Moves to Drop Cases Overturned. Available at: http://www.yorkshirepost.co.uk/news/main-topics/general-news/exclusive-victims-of-crime-

DOI: 10.1057/9781137409270.0012

given-hope-as-moves-to-drop-cases-overturned-1–6383263 Last Accessed: February 2014.

Payne, S. (2009) *Rape: The Victim Experience Review*. Home Office: London.

Perry, B. (2001) *In the Name of Hate: Understanding Hate Crimes*. New York. Routledge.

Pointing, J. and Maguire, M. (1988:1) 'Introduction: The Rediscovery of the Crime Victim' in M. Maguire and J. Pointing (eds) *Victims of Crime: A New Deal?* Milton Keynes: Open University Press.

Quinn, T., Bara, J. and Bartle, J. (2011) 'The UK Coalition Agreement of 2010: Who Won?' *Journal of Elections, Public Opinion & Parties*, 21(2): 295–312.

Respect Taskforce (2006) *Respect Action Plan*. London: Respect Taskforce.

Roberts, J. and Hough, M. (2005) *Understanding Public Attitudes to Criminal Justice*. Oxford: Oxford University Press.

Rock, P. (2007) 'Theoretical Perspectives on Victimisation' in S. Walklate (ed.) The Handbook of Victims and Victimology. Cullompton: Willan.

Rock, P. (1990) *Helping Victims of Crime: The Home Office and the Rise of Victim Support in England and Wales*. Oxford: Clarendon Press.

Rogers, B. (2010) *The Woolwich Model: Can Citizens Tackle Anti-Social Behaviour?* London: The RSA.

Schafer, S. (1968) *The Victim and His Criminal: A Study in Functional Responsibility*. New York: Random House.

Schweppe, J. (2012) 'Defining Characteristics and Politicising Victims: A Legal Perspective', *Journal of Hate Studies*, 10(1): 173–198.

Senior, P. (2013) 'Value for Money? the Politics of Contract Research' in M. Cowburn, M. Duggan, A. Robinson and P. Senior (eds) *Values in Criminology and Community Justice*. Bristol: The Policy Press.

Sentencing Advisory Panel (2005) Advice to the Sentencing Guidelines Council: overarching principles of sentencing. Available at: http://sentencingcouncil.judiciary.gov.uk/docs/web_seriousness_guideline.pdf Last Accessed: February 2014.

Shapland, J., Willmore, J. and P. Duff (1985) *Victims in the Criminal Justice System*. Aldershot: Gower.

Sherry, M. (2010) *Disability Hate Crimes: Does Anybody Really Hate Disabled People?* Farnham: Ashgate.

Smart, C. (1977) *Women, Crime and Criminology*. London: Routledge.

DOI: 10.1057/9781137409270.0012

Social Landlords Crime and Nuisance Group (2013) Reading Behind the Headlines. Available at: http://www.slcng.org.uk/news/1408 Last Accessed: February 2014.

Spalek, B. (2006) *Crime Victims: Theory, Policy, Practice.* Basingstoke: Palgrave Macmillan.

Stanko, E. (1990) *Everyday Violence: How Women and Men Experience Sexual and Physical Danger.* London: Pandora.

Starmer, K. (2013) *The Criminal Justice Response to Child Sexual Abuse: Time for a National Consensus.* London: Crown Prosecution Service.

Stenson, K. (2005) 'Soveriegnty, Biopolitics and the Local Government of Crime in Britain', *Theoretical Criminology*, 9(3):265–287.

Storify (2013) Tom Daley: Homophobia. Available at: http://storify. com/heyjackcooper/tom-daley-homophobia/preview Last Accessed: February 2014.

Taylor-Gooby, P. (2012) 'Root and Branch Restructuring to Achieve Major Cuts: The Social Policy Programme of the 2010 UK Coalition Government', *Social Policy & Administration*, 46(1): 61–82.

The Centre for Social Justice (2009) *Order in the Courts: Restoring Trust through Local Justice.* Available at: http://www.centreforsocialjustice.org. uk/UserStorage/pdf/Pdf%20reports/Order%20in%20the%20Courts.pdf

The Guardian (2013) UK Anti-Muslim Hate Crime Soars, Police Figures Show. Available at: http://www.theguardian.com/society/2013/dec/27/ uk-anti-muslim-hate-crime-soars Last Accessed: February 2014.

The Guardian (2014) Antisocial Behaviour Bill is not the End of the World. Available at: http://www.theguardian.com/society/2014/ jan/08/antisocial-behaviour-bill-not-end-world Last Accessed: February 2014.

The Sun (2009) Scumbag Millionaires: Shamed Bank Boss 'Sorry' for Crisis. REF AS IMAGE DUE TO PAYWALL? Available at: http:// www.thesun.co.uk/sol/homepage/news/money/2225931/Shamed-bank-bosses-sorry-for-crisis.html Last Accessed: March 2014.

Travis, A. (2014) Police Crime Figures Lose Official Status Over Claims of Fiddling. Available at: http://www.theguardian.com/ uk-news/2014/jan/15/police-crime-figures-status-claims-fiddling Last Accessed: February 2014.

Victim Support Website (2010) Victim Support to Deliver New National Victims' Service. Available at: http://www.victimsupport.org.uk/ about-us/news/2010/01/victim-support-to-deliver-new-national-victims-service Last Accessed: February 2014.

DOI: 10.1057/9781137409270.0012

Victim Support Website (2012) Five Promises to Victims and Witnesses: Elected Police and Crime Commissioners. Available at: http://www.victimsupport.org.uk/about-us/campaigns/five-promises/elected-commissioners Last Accessed: February 2014.

von Hentig, H. (1948) *The Criminal and His Victim: Studies in the Socio-Biology of Crime*. Cambridge, MA: Yale University Press.

Walklate, S. (2007) *Imagining the Victim of Crime*. Maidenhead: Open University Press.

Walklate, S. (2011) 'Reframing Criminal Victimization: Finding a Place for Vulnerability and Resilience', *Theoretical Criminology*, 15(2): 179–194.

Watt, P. (2006) 'Respectability, Roughness and "Race": Neighbourhood Place Images and the Making of Working-Class Social Distinctions in London', *International Journal of Urban and Regional Research*, 30(4): 776–797.

Williams, B. (1999) *Working with Victims of Crime: Policies, Politics and Practise*. London: Jessica Kingsley Publishers Ltd.

Wilson, A. (2010) Bankers' Bonus Tax Failed, Admits Alistair Darling. *The Telegraph*. Available at: http://www.telegraph.co.uk/finance/newsbysector/banksandfinance/7976575/Bankers-bonus-tax-failed-admits-Alistair-Darling.html Last Accessed: February 2014.

Wintour, P. (2013) Bedroom Tax Affected More Than 522,000 People, First Figures Show. *The Guardian*. Available at: http://www.theguardian.com/society/2013/nov/13/bedroom-tax-figures-august Last Accessed: February 2014.

Wolfgang, M. (1957) 'Victim Precipitated Criminal Homicide', *Journal of Criminal Law, Criminology and Police Science*, 48(1): 1–11.

Wong, K. (2013) 'The Emperor's New Clothes: Can Big Society Deliver Criminal Justice?' in M. Cowburn, M. Duggan, A. Robinson and P. Senior (eds) *Values in Criminology and Community Justice*. Bristol: The Policy Press.

YouGov (2012) Majority Disapprove of Police and Crime Commissioners Being Supported by Parties. Available at: http://yougov.co.uk/news/2012/10/05/majority-disapprove-police-and-crime-commissioners/ Last Accessed: February 2014.

DOI: 10.1057/9781137409270.0012

Index

DOI: 10.1057/9781137409270.0013